C000130991

VEGETARIAN KETO COOKBOOK

The 2020's Essential Guide To
Vegetarian Ketogenic Diet For Weight
Loss, Cleanse Your Body And Burn Fat.
A Quick And Easy Beginner's Guide To
Low Carb Delicious Food With
Affordable Everyday Keto Recipes.

By

ROSE SMITH

TABLE OF CONTENTS

Vegetarian Keto dinner recipes......................155

INTRODUCTION

The vegetarian diet is universally known as one of the healthiest diet possible. Different studies have discovered that vegetarian diets reduce the probability of serious diseases like heart problems and diabetes. Furthermore, it can help improve health more than the average meat-based diets. However, that doesn't imply that a vegetarian's diet is the best diet for everyone.

The ketogenic diet, for instance, is considered more effective than the vegetarian one for losing weight, emend triglyceride and control the blood sugar levels. If we consider the more severe disease, besides, it can help in reducing the incidence of type two diabetes, obesity, epilepsy, Alzheimer's, various kind of cancer, and polycystic ovary syndrome.

That said, it is undeniable that a ketogenic diet presents some ethical and health issues as well. The first issue arises from all meat-diets, which is the provenance of animal products, like dairy and meat.

Dairy and meat produced from animals raised conventionally, and fed with controlled operations rom, are not just nutritionally inferior, but also contribute to

1

terrific issues like climate change and the abuse of animals. As this wasn't bad enough if the meat you are eating is packaged(e.g., salami, sausages, hot dogs, ham, and bacon), then the risk of type two diabetes, cancer, and heart diseases are dramatically increasing.

Luckily, we can avoid these potential problems by using principles from both the ketogenic and the vegetarian diet. We just need to create an eating plan that is more ethical and healthier not just for humans, but for the environment and the animals too. By doing that, we can get the better out from the vegetarian diet and ketogenic diet to create a unique and healthier diet: the vegetarian ketogenic diet.

WHAT IS THE VEGETARIAN KETOGENIC DIET?

The ketogenic vegetarian diet, as said, unites the keto lifestyle with vegetarianism. The ketogenic diet involves consuming minimal quantities of carbohydrates while eating large amounts of protein and fat in order to bolster the metabolic cycle, called ketosis. Keto diet's primary goal is to lose weight and in particular body fat.

Vegetarianism typically involves the cutting out of poultry, fish, beef, and every other type of meat from your meals, to some degree depending on the person. Vegetarians usually have several explanations for cutting meat, some of which are primarily concerned with health, animal welfare, change in the climate.

Milk and egg are the two major animal foods that may be eaten on the vegetarian ketogenic diet. They are nutrient-dense and have far fewer environmental impacts than chicken, turkey, lamb, beef, farmed salmon, and pork. By sourcing your eggs and milk from local and pasture-raised cattle and chickens, you can bring the beneficial impacts a step further. You are investing in the most ethical and healthiest animal products by supporting these sustainable and healthy livestock rearing traditions.

The problem with a vegetarian keto diet is that most vegetarians are over-dependent on carbohydrates. Even though there are plenty of vegetarian-friendly foods for keto people, the diets based on plants are however different. For various reasons, individuals choose to limit themselves to different animal byproducts.

The other foods permitted is dependent upon your particular form of vegetarianism.

- Ovo-Lacto vegetarians are permitted to consume milk and eggs.
- Ovo vegetarians eat eggs, but they don't eat milk.
- Lacto vegetarians use milk but do not eat eggs.
- Vegans - The vegans eat no animal products, such as eggs and milk (others are insect-derived dyes, honey, and many more).

So many diets claim to be the best for losing weight. The edge benefit of Keto is the so-called ketosis metabolism. Vegetarian keto benefits are nothing to be overlooked.

VEGETARIAN KETO DIET BENEFITS

Everybody aims to have good health without illnesses. Good workouts, healthy living, and following a strict nutritional diet can help you to achieve this. Today, ketogenic and vegetarian diets are two of the major health trends. Of course, these two may not seem to match completely, as the vegetarian diet depends on a large quantity of carbohydrates as the key energy source. However, vegetarians can still pursue a ketogenic lifestyle that can help them to attain both's diets health advantages.

But what are the health advantages of a vegetarian keto diet precisely? By pursuing this, how will your general health improve?

1. Preventing And Combating Diabetes And Obesity.

Studies have shown that the ketogenic diet is a useful method to reduce drugs in diabetes patients. Because the keto-veggie diet restricts carbohydrate consumption and guarantees a sugar-free diet, the blood sugar level is lowered, which reduces the danger of further diabetes considerably. This diet enables those with diabetes to reduce insulin doses or eliminates medications entirely within a couple of weeks.

Besides, a low-carb and sugar-free plant-based diet is a powerful way to make your desired weight loss and maintenance effective. In one research conducted with 164 adolescents, it was determined that a low-carb diet helped them lose weight considerably more quickly, compared to other conventional programs for weight loss. It also increases metabolism, which helps to burn more fat and calories every day.

2. Reducing The Risk Of Heart Disease.

One of the world's major death causes is heart disease. It may be caused by different conditions of health but primarily due to the absence of exercise, obesity, and poor nutrition. Most individuals believe it's not helpful for the heart to have a high-fat diet. Recent researches have shown that the consumption of healthy fats is not only secure but offers long-term health advantages. A constant kéto-veggie diet intake, in comparison to other diets, does not shows any rise in cardiac occurrences. More importantly, it reduces the number of fat molecules and triglycerides circulating in the bloodstream, which are connected to heart disease.

Triglycerides increase when you eat too much carbohydrate that can eventually contribute to a heart condition. If you are following a rigorous keto-veggie diet plan, you should limit your carbohydrate consumption to 50 grams per day. That dramatically reduces blood triglycerides.

3. Enhancing Over-All Mental Health.

Studies demonstrate that keto-veggie nutrition enhances cognitive awareness and improves your critical thinking abilities. Your brain remains youthful and sharp when you follow this lifestyle. With a balanced diet, low carbohydrates but rich with good fats and moderate proteins, protect your neurovascular functions to maintain good cognitive ability. The keto-vegan diet as well contributes to clearing up beta-amyloid protein, which can stay together just to prevent quick and effective signal flows in the brain. Preventing this build-up implies lowering the danger that neurodegenerative illnesses like Alzheimer's will develop.

Since the keto diet was first created for epileptics in the 1920s, surveys indicate that vegetarian ketogenic food can also treat drug-resistant epilepsy. In comparison to other treatments, certain types of epilepsy are safer and cured effectively without problems, hazards, or side impacts.

4. Battling Some Cancer Types.

Despite progress in the sector of medicine, cancer is still difficult to overcome. Today, the majority of cancer treatments have many side effects and health disadvantages. It is not radiation or medication that is the best way to fight cancer. It can be accomplished through adequate metabolism and a healthy lifestyle.

Some researches proved that sugar nourishes cancer cells. The keto-vegan diet removes your system's sugar. Instead of glucose obtained from carbs, ketone cells are used to produce energy. Your system starves cancer cells by decreasing the amount of glucose and carbohydrates. For example, an extremely low-carb diet can reduce the recurrence of certain breast cancer types and can delay brain tumor development.

The keto-veggie diet provides both cancer safety and cancer prevention by minimizing and replacing carbohydrates with good and healthy fats. Reducing starchy vegetable and sugary fruits intake actually causes cancer cells to starve. Many keto-vegan staples help avoid the growth of cancer cells.

5. Helping Vision And Eyesight Improvement.

Keto-veggie diet can help prevent cataracts and glaucoma, progressive illnesses causing bad sight or even blindness. A diet with abundant good fats and low in carbs can contribute to healthy retinal cells and also prevent degeneration of the cells.

8

As the keto-veggie diet prevents diabetes, it also reduces the prospective connections with glaucoma. Even individuals with glaucoma can improve their sight and delay or even prevent the development of the disease.

6. Providing Good Stomach and Gut Health.

The keto-veggie diet has a diverse and healthy intestinal microbiome. A healthy intestine with lots of good bacteria will make your body more effective in absorbing fats and nutrients. These beneficial bacteria assist you in getting a robust intestinal cover, which helps to break down meals and stimulates the absorption of nutrients. Some bacteria in our stomach also assist in providing the body with vitamin B12 and K. Those vitamins are crucial for the regulation of minerals, such as calcium, in our collection.

In other words, this diet guarantees proper metabolism. An unbalanced stomach microbiome can affect your metabolic frequency. An unhealthy intestine may result in illness and even an increase in weight.

7. Stabilizes Hormones

Hormones are the body's chemical transmitters. It could be messy to have hormonal imbalances. Ketosis has an excellent influence on your hormones. This process reduces your body's insulin concentrations by removing your dietary sugar. Apart from that, leptin (a sort of hormone that reduces hunger) levels are decreased and help to control your eating patterns.

This diet enables the pituitary gland, which controls progesterone and the thyroid, to work better in women. That will helps to prevent progesterone deficiency and infertility.

8. Providing Higher Levels Of Energy For The Day.

You may feel bored with the high consumption of carbohydrates. If you eat high carbs for food (for instance, pizza), the starches in the food are split into glucose. Your body needs insulin in this process to take glucose out of the bloodstream. This energy is required for our body functions. After surplus carbohydrates have been consumed, an energy spike will be achieved, but a considerable decrease will follow rapidly and make you weary and tired after meals.

You will not meet any of these problems in a vegetarian keto diet. Your body now relies on fats rather than carbohydrates. It will not take carbohydrate energy. Excessive manufacturing of insulin is avoided because your body can now always use stored fat. You will thus experience a steady stream of energy all day long.

9. Making Skin Healthier And Clearer.

Reducing your system's carbohydrates will make skin clearer. Besides dairy foods, simple carbohydrates can also trigger inflammation, one of the significant causes of acne.

A highly glycemic diet can exacerbate acne and often lead to breakouts. While it is recognized that sugar and carbs cause pimples, healthy fats calm dry skin on the contrary and discourage inflammatory acne. So, this diet is for you if you want a brighter, smoother, and shining skin.

10. Enhancing Sleep.

The keto-veggie diet also will help improve sleep. One significant advantage of following this diet is that it enables you to be alert during the day and to relax in the evening. Patterns for sleep shift because carbs are reduced, and healthy fats are increased. Researchers indicate that the keto-veggie diet may influence brain chemical called adenosine, which helps to regulate sleep.

It is no surprise why people all over the world begin to use the ketogenic diet in their lifetime. As already stated, the demonstrated advantages are numerous: loss of weight (especially around the abdomen), control of blood sugar, better energy, improved endurance. The vegetarian ketogenic diet is comparable, except that it eliminates some animal products from the keto diet. By doing that it mix possibly the beneficial impacts both vegetarian and ketogenic diets and decreasing disease danger from cooked food and red meat. There is almost no research on a ketogenic vegetarian diet; the long-term impacts have still to be researched. However, anecdotal evidence is available from individuals who thrive on this kind of diet.

MAKING THE KETO DIET VEGETARIAN

Keto dieters should chop down all grains, legumes and high-carbon fruit and vegetables to help reduce carb consumption. Ketones are also urged to increase their consumption of fatty milk products, fatty meat cuts, oily fish, and seed and nuts. Ketones must also remain mild with foods rich in protein, such as eggs, meat cuts, substitutes of meat and fruits and vegetables of low-carb.

So how do you create this vegetarian diet when you look at these guidelines? After all, a variety of vegetarian staples like fruit and grain are excluded from the menu. Well, a vegetarian keto diet is feasible with some research and thorough planning. Here are several methods of making the keto diet vegetarian and nutritious:

1) Eat enough protein.

With keto, the amount of protein needed per kilogram of body weight is around 0.8 grams. By substituting meat for other protein-rich foods, you can readily fulfill minimum protein demands. Good choices include high-fat dairy products; nutritionists argue that the highest sources of high-quality protein are probably milk products. That is due to the fact that all nine essential amino acids in dairy proteins are more uncomplicated to digest than either soy or beef proteins. Make sure you go for fatty products to make them more keto. Examples are cheese, sour cream, and fat yogurt.

Pastured Eggs - Eggs are one of the most excellent sources of protein accessible immediately after milk. If possible, go pasture because they are nutritious more than conventional eggs. A big egg contains approximately 6.3 grams of protein with all vital amino acids and 24 grams of fat, making it suitable for keto.

Nuts And Seeds - Most of them are protein-rich. However, not all the vital amino acids are typically contained. That's why a range of nuts and seeds are needed to make sure you satisfy your requirements for protein. Among the alternatives on keto are almonds, sesame seeds, walnuts, hazelnuts, pistachios, and chia seeds. You should also have nut butter on the food list for keto.

Tofu and Meat Substitutes - Soy products in the Keto society are somewhat contentious. Some dietitians argue that antinutrients and phytoestrogens in soy can have an adverse health and diet impact. On the other hand, soy is an uncommon plant source of all essential amino acids which make it a valued food that is vegan. While the number of carbs of soy milk may be high, tofu contains only approximately 2 grams of carbs net in 7oz.

2) Eat 3 Low-Carb Portions Of Vegetables.

Keto does not allow grains and legumes, but low-carb vegetables are definitely permitted. To fulfill your daily requirements for vitamins, minerals, and fiber, you have to eat at least three servings of vegetables every day. Vegetables also have many phytochemicals to benefit health and study has shown that your danger of heart attack, cancer, and cognitive deterioration is reduced.

Examples of low-carb vegetables are:

- Leafy greens: kale, parsley, cabbage, lettuce, endive, celery, spinach, arugula, and broccoli.
- Above-ground vegetables: cauliflower, cucumbers, asparagus, zucchini, peppers, and eggplants.

3) Stick With Low-Carb Fruit And Berries.

The fruit is the candy of nature and is certainly not permitted on keto. However, there are a few exceptions. Berries are typically low in carbs, and you can occasionally enjoy many other low-carb keto fruits. Use fruit to make your Keto desserts taste better, but keep an eye on your carb count.

4) Eat Several Different Fats.

Fat will represent the majority of your food, so choosing the healthiest and highest quality fats accessible is essential. You also need a range of fats to guarantee that you give your body all it requires. Some fats are vital, but others are not. Some fats also add value to your health, while others put you at risk of disease.

SOME TIPS BEFORE YOU GET STARTED

Tip 1 - Don't hesitate on the same day to exchange breakfast for dinner or breakfast for lunch. If you like, you might as well swap entire days. Look at the proposed replacement options if you do not love certain ingredients.

Tip 2 - If you just cook, freeze or cool the rest of your portions or halve the recipes when needed (e.g., freeze half Keto Pasta for next week).

Tip 3 - In the refrigerator, have some hard-boiled eggs prepared for snacks or recipes. Usually, no snacks should be required between meals. But, if you do, make sure you have some keto-friendly snacks at your disposal (eggs, cheese, nuts, etc.).

Tip 4 - Magnesium is often deficient in very low carb diets (less than 30 grams of net carbohydrate). I suggest that you take supplements of magnesium, or add magnesium-high snacks like nuts. If you have any signs of keto-flu, ensure that you consume extra sodium and decrease the portion of dairy and eggs if you need less protein. Don't think too hard about little protein excess as it isn't going to get you out of ketosis. Protein, in reality, maintains starvation. When adding more (or less) fat, concentrate your adjustments on added oils and fatty foods.

Tip 5 - Take all three macro parts of your food, taking into account the suggested proportions (5% carbs, 25% protein, 70% fat) for your ketogenic intake. In this manner, you understand that you get all the nutrients you need while also ensuring you get into ketosis and remain in it.

Tip 6 - Snack on low-carb sweets, seeds, and nuts. Nuts and seeds are an ideal source of major macros and fiber in a vegetarian diet. Just watch your carbohydrate consumption when you enjoy these low-carb and high-fat snacks. It certainly helps to use applications such as MyFitnessPal.

Tip 7 - Make yourself creative with the substitute. You do not need to give up your favorite food simply because you are on a low-carb diet. Stevia-sweetened desserts, zucchini noodles, avocado spreads, rice cauliflower, and almond flour muffins are some of your favorite dishes that offer great low-carbon twists.

Tip 8 - If they assist satisfy your macros, do not shy back from a couple of processed foods. Usually, you will hear that the way to go on keto is to exclude processed food. Although this is a wise thing, following a more restricted version in the ketogenic diet may cause you some trouble. Adding TVP, trans-free margarine, and canned products can be a useful way to get your vegetarian ketogenic diet with all the nutrients you need while being low in carbohydrate and rich in good fats.

Tip 9 - Choose low carbohydrates and fatty vegetables whenever possible. You can enjoy several low-carb fruits on your vegetarian ketogenic diet. Some fat examples can be found too, the most remarkable being an avocado. When you eat these foods, please make sure you keep track of your carbohydrates, as it is easy for you to overboard the diet with carbs.

Tip 10 - If necessary, supplement. Among many other ketos, supplements are exogenous ketones, collagen peptides, and MCT oil. It helps you satisfy your macros, achieve ketosis, and feel comfortable with a keto diet. Add your own favorite supplement to enhance your vegetarian ketogenic diet.

Tip 11 - Finally, if you're not famished, don't eat, even if it implies you're going to skip a meal.

FOODS TO EAT

You likely wonder how to bring this into exercise now that you understand what foods you need to be careful about on your vegetarian ketogenic diet. At first, it can look tricky to make vegetarian dishes. But you will build a collection of vegetarian recipes with a little researching and practice so that your diet is both nutritious and enjoyable.

Let us begin with listing some essential components that you must add to your refrigerator and cupboard:

Plant-based fats: Olives and its oils, avocados and its oil, coconut and its oil (but do not eat any sweetened coconut).

Low-carb vegetarian proteins: Seitan, tofu, and even tempeh; even if it is higher in carbs than tofu and seitan, it is also higher in fiber, which makes your net carbs keto-friendly. Be cautious about faux-meat burgers, bacon, etc. and check their list of ingredients and nutrition tags as they can contain sugar or as an unwanted carbs source.

Low-carb vegetables: Cauliflower of course, and also asparagus, swiss chard, brussels sprouts, cabbage, mushrooms, zucchini, broccoli rabe, spinach, bok choy, kale, and lettuces (romaine, arugula, green and red leaf, endive, and so on).

Nuts: When you eat vegetarian keto, every nut is the right choice, but some are higher in fat and lower in carbohydrates than the others, and these are pili nuts, macadamias, hazelnuts, and pecans.

Seeds: Here, you can't really go wrong. Seeds are fatty, not too high in carbohydrates and ordinarily full of fiber, which can cause your net carbs to fall.

Dairy: Hard cheeses, butter, full-fat plain yogurt, and plain cottage cheese (avoid the flavored high-sugar varieties).

Eggs: This is the easiest, healthiest, and most excellent way to get protein if you eat vegetarian keto. Eggs also give you a good dose of fat and almost no carbs.

Berries: Blackberries, strawberries, and raspberries all offer lower carb fruit choices. Not because they really have low carbohydrates, but because they have fiber and therefore your net carbohydrates are low. You may want to avoid blueberries because a cup will eat almost all of your daily carb allotment.

Condiments and spices: Soy sauce (light), apple cider vinegar (ACV), basil pesto, mayonnaise, mustard, hot sauce, ranch dressing, all spices, and herbs.

And, as valuable as it is to have a list of foods you can consume, you might also wish to list the foods you cannot eat (those foods that will throw you out of the status of ketosis), in order to successfully use a vegetarian ketogenic diet. These are legumes, cereals, most fruit and all kinds of potatoes.

While the keto diet cuts down on many food groups on which vegetarian depend, such as starchy vegetables and whole grains, cautious scheduling can be used to follow a vegetarian keto diet. Vegetarians should obtain their calories from whole and unprocessed foods while evading highly manufactured vegetarian meals.

FOODS TO AVOID

You should stay away from all meat and seafood in a vegetarian keto diet. High carbohydrates foods such as cereals, legumes, starchy vegetables, and fruit can only be allowed in tiny quantities, provided that they match your regular carb allotment.

The following foods have to be removed:

- Fish and shellfish: salmon, tuna, sardines, anchovies, and lobster
- Poultry: chicken, turkey, duck, and goose
- Meat: beef, pork, lamb, goat, and veal

Here are certain foods you should restrict:

- Sweeteners: brown sugar, white sugar, honey, maple syrup, and agave nectar
- Sugar-sweetened beverages: soda, sweet tea, sports drinks, juice, and energy drinks
- Starchy vegetables: potatoes, yams, beets, parsnips, carrots, and sweet potatoes
- Fruits: apples, bananas, oranges, berries, melon, apricots, plums, and peaches
- Grains: bread, rice, quinoa, oats, millet, rye, barley, buckwheat, and pasta
- Processed foods: breakfast cereals, granola, chips, cookies, crackers, and baked goods
- Legumes: beans, peas, lentils, and chickpeas
- Condiments: barbecue sauce, honey mustard, ketchup, marinades, and sweetened salad dressings
- Alcoholic beverages: beer, wine, and sweetened cocktails

WHOLE GRAIN SHOW

It is no news that whole grains possess more fibers that provides longer enduring satiety and improved digestion and maintain their bran and germ, which are their highest nutrient-rich parts, once milled into flours.

It could take you a while to settle to whole grain treatments when you eat refined flour-based goodies. As your palate adjusts to the flavor of whole grain, a mild flavor and a wide variety of exquisite flavors and texture will be discovered. Allow your taste buds to speak. You may have the same reaction that we did, and ask yourselves why you have ever spent time and cash on flours, which is obviously not healthy.

Some of the flours that are described in this book are not the type you can collect in the convenient local shop, but they can be found easily in well-stocked natural food stores, specialty stores, or online. I would suggest that the flour be bought in bulk and stored in containers that are airtight in the refrigerator, or preferably in a freezer. Allow the powder to reach the room temperature for about 15 minutes before starting to bake, and remember to return the container to the refrigerator as soon as possible. As always, when accessible and inexpensive, we support organic flours (and ingredients generally).

All flours have distinct properties and give baked goods their own attributes. I cannot, therefore, recommend the use of alternatives to the flours in my recipes. If you do

22

this, the result may not be as pleasant as it should be. Continue to read for a more in-depth look.

Teff flour: Teff meal is best used in Ethiopian flatbread injera. The flour is light, gluten-free and has an unparalleled sweet malty flavor.

Amaranth flour: Amaranth is a slightly nutty, malty, buttery high-protein flour. It is best utilized in small quantities. It needs to be coupled with other flours in order to produce baked goods with a correct structure because it does not have gluten.

Oats flour: Oats flour are available in several varieties. They taste nice, and the textures of the different grinds provide a different baking element. Oatmeal has a delicious, tender crumb in quick bread, whereas old-fashioned rolled oats have dreadful texture in yeasted bread. By grinding old fashioned or even quick-cooking oats in a food processor or blender, you can make your own oat flour.

Brown fice flour: Brown rice flour in its flavor is mildly nutty. Some people think it's awful, but I have had luck with Bob's fine-ground brand. This flour is gluten-free as well.

Buckwheat flour: Buckwheat flour is protein-rich, gluten-free, nutty and hearty. In contrast to a brighter variant, the dark-colored kind has fewer hull colors.

Millet flour: Millet flour is a flexible, non-gluten flour that is suitable for use in any non-yeasted baking in conjunction with other flours. It can also be assorted with wheat flour to generate yeast breads with low gluten content.

Rye flour: Rye flour includes some gluten, but can produce too thick baked products when used in large amounts. The flour of pumpernickel is more rooted in color, coarser than other rye flours and has a more distinct flavor. If one type of these two meals can only be found, you can replace the other one because the contrast will not be visible.

Barley flour: Barley flour has a very gentle flavor that makes it glow when combined with other ingredients. This is a flour with low gluten that when combined with the other flours improves soft crumb texture.

Rolled flakes: Rolled flakes are made from whole grains, which are steamed, roasted, ground, and flaked. They have the characteristic taste of the grain from which they are made. If you don't have access to Kamut, spelt, or rye flakes, use the more readily available old-fashioned oats in their place.

Graham flour: This is coarse whole wheat flour that works wonders in baked goods. It can easily be replaced with whole wheat pastry flour (in anything that isn't yeast bread) or any sort of whole wheat flour (white whole wheat or regular), if unavailable where you live. Do not confuse it with gram flour, which is made from chickpeas!

Rolled flakes: Rolled flakes are produced from whole grains that are gone, flaked, steamed and roasted. They adopt the flavor properties of the grain they are produced from. Use the most easily accessible old-fashioned oats as a substitute if you do not have access to spelt, Kamut and rye flakes.

Graham Flour: This is coarse entire wheat flour that works wonderfully well in baked products. The whole wheat pastry flour or any kind of whole wheat flour can readily be substituted if not available where you reside. Don't mistake it with gram flour made from chickpea!

Whole wheat pastry flour: Whole wheat flour is loony and tasty as all wheat meal and is now a go-too flour for any baking that requires no yeast. It operates well in conjunction with all powders. It is ideal for stuff like cakes and muffins because it produces light outcomes compared to standard whole grain bread.

Cornmeal, cornflour, and cornstarch: Cornmeal is available in multiple grinds. In quick bread, individuals prefer to use fine, however, to maintain the ground or coarse version for other applications. Coarse maize carries with it a toothy crunch along with the sweet undercurrent cornmeal is renowned for, while the cornflour provides baked goods with a cakelike texture. This meal is gluten-free and should be used for improved structure with other flours. Cornstarch is made from ground corn and as well a thickening agent and binder. I highly suggest that you buy the non-genetically altered type, as with all foods.

Whole spelt flour: A cousin of wheat is sweet spelt flour with a nutty flavor. Protein and gluten are high, but gluten is fussier than ordinary wheat. This flour absorbs water differently from other flours, especially between various products. Bob's Red Mill and Arrowhead Mills have been discovered to be the most stable. Note that Red Mills from Bob tend to need more liquid than the Mills from Arrowhead. However, you will have success with all products if you take your time and obey the instructions and add flour when necessary. Notice that various kinds or classes of spelt flour are present, which vary in their quantity of bran. Whole sprinkled meal, also called "light spelt meal," includes little to no bran and therefore has lower nutrients. And what we call in our dishes is a white sprinkled meal.

White or regular whole wheat flour: White whole wheat flour is made out of hard white spring wheat, while red wheat is made with traditional whole wheat flour. These two meals can be used interchangeably so that, if a recipe requires whole wheat flour, you should be aware that you can instead use full wheat flour without having to have a beat. Many people prefer a more mild taste and a lighter white whole wheat flour than regular whole wheat flour. They come in different grinds like all the flours. I prefer the thin ground that looks similar to the all-purpose meal. Grosser grinds will still function but need more time to absorb liquids.

ONE-WEEK VEGETARIAN KETO MEAL PLAN

Note that no additional snacks are included in the nutrition data of this meal plan. With different personal demands, you can add tasty meals to your appetite from this list. Simply put, add fat and protein-based food or snacks if you're starving.

While the diet of vegetarian keto may seem very restrained, many dishes can be made with vegan foods. A sample schedule for a vegetarian keto diet for a week follows:

DAY 1

Breakfast - Vegan Keto Porridge
Total carbs: 5,78 g; Protein: 17,82 g; Fat: 13,07 g; Calories: 249 kcal

Lunch - Portobello Mushrooms Tacos (2 Portions)
Total carbs: 83,00 g; Protein: 18,8 g; Fat: 22,6 g, Calories: 614 kcal

Dinner - Tofu Nuggets (2 portions)
Total carbs: 44,8 g; Protein: 23,4 g; Fat: 17,6 g; Calories:
268 kcal

DAY 2

*Breakfast - Charred Veggie and Fried Goat Cheese
Salad*
Total carbs: 7,08 g; Protein: 16,09 g; Fat: 27,61 g;
Calories: 350 kcal

Lunch - Vegan Butter Pecan Sandwich (2 Portions)
Total carbs: 28,00 g; Protein: 40,00 g; Fat: 27,6 g;
Calories: 490 kcal

Dinner - Artichoke Spinach Casserole
Total carbs: 7,00 g; Protein: 37.,00 g; Fat: 35,00 g;
Calories: 493 kcal

DAY 3

Breakfast - Super Eggy Vegan Tofu Scramble
Total carbs: 3,8 g; Protein: 20,3 g; Fat: 13,1 g; Calories:
206 kcal

*Lunch - Riced Cauliflower Stir-Fry & Crispy Peanut
Tofu*
Total carbs: 38,5 g; Protein: 24,5 g; Fat: 34,00 g;
Calories: 524 kcal

Dinner - Tikka Masala
Total carbs: 4,8 g; Protein: 24,8 g; Fat: 21,00 g; Calories:
302 kcal

DAY 4

Breakfast - Fluffy Low Carb Blueberry Pancakes (2 Portions)
Total carbs: 8,2 g; Protein: 14,00 g; Fat: 14,00 g;
Calories: 264 kcal

Lunch - Baked Parmesan Zucchini Rounds (2 Portions)
Total carbs: 14,00 g; Protein: 22,00 g; Fat: 14,00 g;
Calories: 282 kcal

Dinner - Vegan Hemp Heart Porridge (2 Portions)
Total carbs: 18,00 g; Protein: 22,00 g; Fat: 66,00 g;
Calories: 718 kcal

DAY 5

Breakfast - No-bake Vegan Pecan Pie Bars (3 Portions)
Total carbs: 5,00 g; Protein: 5,00 g; Fat: 16 g; Calories:
175 kcal

Lunch - Sesame Carrot Falafel (3 Portions)
Total carbs: 34,8 g; Protein: 16,2 g; Fat: 67,5 g; Calories:
876 kcal

Dinner - Spaghetti Squash
Total carbs: 20,00 g; Protein: 13,6 g; Fat: 20,00 g;
Calories: 277 kcal

DAY 6

Breakfast - Grilled Cheese Sandwich

Total carbs: 6,14 g; Protein: 25,84 g; Fat: 69,95 g; Calories: 803 kcal

Lunch - Vegan Burrata & Roasted Cauliflower (2 Portions)

Total carbs: 10,00 g; Protein: 18,00 g; Fat: 22,00 g; Calories: 300 kcal

Dinner - Baked Badrijani (2 Portions)

Total carbs: 11,4 g; Protein: 8,00 g; Fat: 64,16 g; Calories: 668 kcal

DAY 7

Breakfast - Low Carb Vegan Pancakes
Total carbs: 13,9 g; Protein: 9,6 g; Fat: 20,8 g; Calories: 259,6 kcal

Lunch - Lunch Tofu Scramble (3 Portions)
Total carbs: 6,3 g; Protein: 27,9 g; Fat: 14,1 g; Calories: 330 kcal

Dinner - Vegan Strawberry Chia Jars (2 Portions)
Total carbs: 15,00 g; Protein: 17,4 g; Fat: 35,8 g; Calories: 460 kcal

RECIPE SOBSTITUTIONS

If you don't like some ingredients, or if you're intolerant with certain foods, you can make some changes. You can use cocoa milk, rather than cream, or more eggs rather than cheese if you don't consume dairy.

In substitution of a Keto Bun: 1 low-carb bagel or 1-2 slices of Rye bread or some Keto Buns without nuts.

You can utilize other alternatives for breakfast, such as pancakes and granola. In these pages, I have tried to minimize delicious food and to only include fast breakfast, particularly during weekdays.

The use of such options does not alter nutrition facts considerably. Nevertheless, be aware that without substitutions, the shopping list is created.

VEGETARIAN KETO BREAKFAST RECIPES

The best ideas for an healthy breakfast, using keto and vegetarian recipes that are easy and tasty! Easy, quiky and grab-and-go breakfast recipes which can be made in advance, freezer-friendly and 100% low carb! Keto-friendly breakfasts just need to fulfill the keto diet principles- Low carb, low sugar and packed with healthy fats and protein!

FLOURLESS BANANA BREAD

The best healthy banana bread recipe made with almond flour! Tender on the outside, moist and fluffy on the inside, this healthy banana breakfast bread is paleo, vegan, gluten-free, and sugar-free!

Ingredients

- 1/4 tsp salt
- 2 tbsp granulated sweetener of choice
- 1/2 cup coconut oil
- 2 cups blanched almond flour
- 1 tsp vanilla extract
- 2 flax eggs (Vegan Version) or 2 whole eggs
- 1 tsp baking powder
- 1 tsp cinnamon
- 2 large overripe bananas, mashed

Instructions

1. Preheat your oven to about 350°F. Grease and put aside a 10x 10 inch square pan.
2. Combine the dry ingredients and blend well in a big mixing bowl.
3. Melt your coconut oil in a separate bowl. Add and whisk together your flaxed eggs/regular eggs and mashed bananas.
4. Combine the blend wet and dry and blend until it is fully integrated. Pour into the already greased saucepan.

5. Bake for about 40-50 minutes or until a toothpick comes out smoothly from the center (square pan tends to take about 40-minute to bake while loaf pans take roughly 45-50 minutes to cook).
6. Leave the food in the pan to cool for about 10 minutes before transferring it to a wire rack where it is completely cooled off. Slice and enjoy your meal.

Nutrition Facts

Serves: 1 serving / Calories: 142kcal /
Carbohydrates: 8g / Protein: 12g / Fat: 8g

BLUEBERRY BREAKFAST CAKE

A delightful breakfast cake recipe that is fast and simple to make; the recipe is loaded with blueberries and filled with a lot of protein! Perfect for the preparation of meals, it is keto-friendly and has a vegan and flourless option.

Ingredients

Original Recipe:

- 1 tbsp cinnamon
- 1/4 cup unsweetened applesauce
- 1 tsp baking soda
- 1 cup blueberries
- 1/4 cup coconut flour
- 2 cups blanched almond flour
- 3 large eggs
- 1/4 cup sticky sweetener of choice
- 1/4 cup coconut oil

Vegan/Flourless Recipe:

- 1 tsp vanilla extract
- Pinch sea salt
- 1 T baking powder
- 1 cup milk of choice
- 1/4-1/2 cup blueberries
- 1/2 cup coconut palm sugar (alternatively, you can use any granulated sweetener of choice)
- 6 T smooth almond butter (alternatively, you can use any nut or seed butter of choice)
- 1 flax egg (Vegan Version) or 1 large egg
- 2 cups gluten-free rolled oats ground into a flour

Instructions

For the original recipe:

1. Preheat your oven to about 350°F. Line the loaf pan or square pan to use with parchment paper and set the pan aside.
2. Using a large mixing bowl, add all your dry ingredients and mix them well.
3. Whisk your eggs as well in a completely different bowl. Then add your unsweetened apple sauce, sticky sweetener of choice, and melted coconut oil, and mix it very well.
4. Combine all of your wet and dry ingredients and mix very well again. Fold the product of the mixture through your blueberries.
5. Transfer your blueberry cake batter into the square pan and bake for 35-40 minutes or until a dry and clean toothpick comes out of the center of the cake. Let it cool while it is in the pan for about 10 minutes, then fully cool it down by transferring it to a wire rack.
6. When the cake has completely cooled off, prepare your frosting before topping up the cake and then cutting it into slices.

For the flourless/vegan recipe:

1. Using a high-speed blender, combine all the ingredients and blend well until you get a smooth batter. Follow the guidelines above.

Nutrition Facts

Serves: 1 serving / Calories: 135kcal /
Carbohydrates: 7g / Protein: 8g / Fat: 11g

LOW CARB CARROT CAKE

A delightful and perfectly suitable breakfast meal of healthy flourless carrot cake recipe filled healthy fat, protein, and wholesome carbohydrates. This carrot cake is entirely gluten-free, dairy-free, vegan, and sugar-free; also tender on the outside and fluffy and filling inside!

Ingredients

Healthy Low Carb Carrot Cake Recipe

- 1 tsp almond extract (alternatively 1 tsp vanilla extract)
- 1/2 cup tapioca flour
- 2 medium bananas, overripe
- 2 large eggs
- 2 tbsp coconut flour
- 1 tbsp cinnamon
- 1/3 cup olive oil can (alternatively 1/3 cup vegetable or canola oil)
- 1 + 1/2 cups shredded carrots (3 large carrots)
- 1 tsp baking soda
- 1 + 1/4 cups blanched almond flour
- 1 tsp nutmeg
- 1/2 cup granulated sweetener of choice

Vegan and Eggless Carrot Cake Option (Banana-free)

- 1/3 cup chopped walnuts
- 1 1/4 cups gluten-free flour sifted
- 1 tbsp cinnamon
- 2 tbsp unsweetened shredded coconut
- 1 tbsp apple cider vinegar
- 1 1/4 cups blanched

- almond flour
- 3/4 cup milk of choice
- 1/2 cup pure maple syrup
- 1 medium carrot, shredded
- 1/4 tsp baking soda
- 1 tsp nutmeg
- 1/4 cup olive oil (alternatively 1/4 cup vegetable or canola oil)

Instructions

For the low carb carrot cake:

1. Preheat your oven to about 350°F. Line the loaf pan or square pan to use with a parchment paper and set it aside.
2. Combine all your dry ingredients except the granulated sweetener in a large mixing bowl and mix it well.
3. In another small mixing bowl, add your eggs, almond extract, olive oil and granulated sweetener of choice and mix it as well.
4. Combine the wet and the dry mixture and mix them together. Add your mashed banana and mix it well. Now add your shredded carrots and continue to mix until fully incorporated.
5. Transfer the carrot cake batter in the lined pan and allow it bake for 45-50 minutes, or until a dry and clean toothpick comes out from the center.
6. Cool it by leaving it the pan for about 10 minutes, then transfer it to a wire rack to fully cool off. Once it is cold, top the cake with frosting and enjoy.

For the vegan and eggless option:

1. Preheat your oven to about 350°F. Line the loaf pan or square pan to use with a parchment paper and set it aside.
2. Combine your apple cider vinegar, olive oil, maple syrup, and milk of choice in a large mixing bowl and mix everything them together. Add in your walnuts, shredded coconut, and shredded carrots and mix lightly.
3. Add your baking soda, blanched almond flour, sifted flour, and spices and mix it well. If the batter becomes too thick, supplement it with more milk.
4. Transfer the carrot cake batter in the lined pan and let it bake for about 25-35 minutes until golden brown and a toothpick come out clean from the center of the cake. Note that the baking times will depend on how big your loaf pan is.
5. Leave it in the pan to cool for about 10 minutes, then transfer it to a wire rack to fully cool off. Once it is cold, top the cake with frosting and enjoy.

Nutrition Facts

Serves: 1 serving / Calories: 153kcal /
Carbohydrates: 3.5g / Protein: 3g / Fat: 7g

LOW CARB OATMEAL

A fast and easy to make recipe produced with chia seeds, flaxseed, and unsweetened coconut flakes for low carb keto overnight oatmeal! Alternative little carb oatmeal packed with fiber, protein, and made with about 4-5 ingredients.

Ingredients

- 1/2 cup hot liquid of choice (I used water)
- 1/2 cup cold liquid of choice (I used unsweetened coconut milk)
- 2 tbsp granulated sweetener of choice
- 2 tbsp ground flaxseed
- 2 tbsp unsweetened shredded coconut
- 2 tbsp chia seeds

Instructions

1. Using a small mixing bowl, add all your dry ingredients and mix them properly.
2. Add half a cup of the hot liquid of your choice and mix it well (the mixture should be super thick). Add your cold liquid of choice and mix until a thick, creamy 'oatmeal' remains.
3. Once it is cold, add toppings or mix-ins of your choice and enjoy it.

Nutrition Facts

Serves: 1 serving / Calories: 250kcal /
Carbohydrates: 16g / Protein: 8g / Fat: 17g

NO-BAKE CASHEW COCONUT BARS

An easy and quick to make a recipe for homemade keto no-bake cashew coconut bars! It is filled with protein and made sugar free, meaning it is made without sugar or dates.

Ingredients

- 2 tbsp shredded coconut
- 2 cups raw cashews
- 1/4 cup chia seeds
- 1 cup almond butter
- 1 cup granulated sweetener of choice
- 1/4 cup liquid of choice
- 1 cup raw almonds

Instructions

1. Line the 8 x 8-inch freezer-friendly pan to use with a parchment paper and set it aside.
2. Combine your cashews and almonds with a high-speed blender or any food processor accessible and blend it until you get a crumbly texture.
3. Add your almond chia seeds, granulated sweetener, and butter and blend it very well, until a thick, gooey batter remains. If the dough becomes too thick, supplement it with more milk or any liquid of your choice.
4. Transfer the cashew coconut no-bake bar batter into the lined square pan. Drizzle the mixture

with some coconut and place it in the freezer. When they become firm, cut into bars and keep it frozen.

Nutrition Facts

Serves: 1 serving / Calories: 175kcal / Carbohydrates: 6g / Protein: 5g / Fat: 17g

NO-BAKE PECAN PIE BARS

A healthy and very easy to put together vegan recipe loaded with pecans and packed with flavor. It has a super low amount of carbohydrates and no sugar!

Ingredients

- 2 cups pecans
- 1/4 cup chia seeds
- 1 cup granulated sweetener of choice
- 1/4 cup milk of choice
- 1 cup almond butter, can use any nut or seed butter
- 1 cup almonds
- 1/4 cup chocolate chips (optional)

Instructions

1. Line the inside of your 8 x 8-inch freezer-friendly pan with a parchment paper and set it aside.
2. Combine your pecans and almonds with a high-speed blender or any food processor accessible and blend it until you get a crumbly texture.
3. Add your almond chia seeds, granulated sweetener, and almond butter and blend it very well, until a thick, gooey batter remains. If the dough becomes too crumbly, supplement it with more milk or any liquid of your choice.
4. Turn over the pecan pie batter from the bowl into the lined square pan and use your hand to press

it firmly to hold it into place. Include some chocolate chips if you want and refrigerate until it is solidified. Use a mildly wet knife to cut it into bars and enjoy.

Nutrition Facts

Serves: 1 serving | Calories: 175kcal / Carbohydrates: 5g / Protein: 5g / Fat: 16g

FLUFFY LOW CARB BLUEBERRY PANCAKES

This recipe of thick and fluffy keto blueberry pancakes is prepared with almond flour and coconut flour. These keto pancakes come with a no-flour and dairy-free version, and it is flawless for those on a vegan, sugar-free, paleo and low carb diet!

Ingredients

Low Carb Version

- 1/4 cup fresh blueberries (thawed frozen ones work best)
- 1/2 cup almond flour
- 3 large eggs
- 2 tbsp coconut flour
- 1/2 tsp baking powder
- 1/4 cup milk of choice
- 1 tsp cinnamon
- 1-2 tbsp granulated sweetener of choice

Flourless Version

- 1 medium banana
- 1 tbsp baking powder
- 1/4-1/2 cup milk of choice
- 1 tbsp apple cider vinegar
- 1 tbsp sticky sweetener of choice
- 1/2 tsp vanilla extract
- 1 cup rolled oats
- 1/2 cup fresh blueberries (thawed frozen ones work best)

Instructions

1. Mix all your ingredients, except for the blueberries, in a high-speed blender or any food processor accessible and blend it until you get a thick batter.
2. Find a large mixing bowl and turn your batter into it and then continue to stir the mixture through your blueberries. Stop shaking and allow your dough to sit for about 5-10 minutes, to become thick. If the batter becomes too thick, supplement it with more milk or any liquid of your choice.
3. Grease a large non-stick pan and preheat it over low/medium heat. When the pan is hot, pour one-quarter of the whole batter onto the pan and cover it immediately. Let the pancakes cook for 2-3 minutes and when the edges are golden, flip it and repeat this process with the rest of the batter.
4. Serve instantly once cooked or allow it to cool before freezing or refrigerating it for later use.

Nutrition Facts

Serves: 1 serving / Calories: 132kcal /
Carbohydrates: 4.1g / Protein: 7g / Fat: 7g

FLUFFY LOW CARB CINNAMON ROLL PANCAKES

This recipe is thick and fluffy low carb cinnamon roll pancakes, and it comes with two options! One is without flour and without egg, and the other uses coconut flour and almond flour to produce a keto-friendly recipe.

Ingredients

Low Carb Version

- 1/4 cup milk of choice
- 1/2 cup almond flour
- 2 tbsp coconut flour
- 1-2 tbsp granulated sweetener of choice
- 3 large eggs
- 1 tsp cinnamon
- 1/2 tsp baking powder

Flourless Version

- 1 tsp vanilla
- 1/2 cup unsweetened applesauce (alternatively pumpkin, banana or sweet potato)
- 1/4-1/2 cup milk of choice
- 1 tbsp sticky sweetener of choice
- 1 tsp baking powder
- 1 tsp cinnamon
- 1 cup rolled oats (Alternatively quinoa flakes)
- 1 tbsp apple cider vinegar (Alternatively lemon or lime juice)

49

For the sticky cinnamon roll glaze

- 1 tsp cinnamon
- 1-2 tbsp coconut butter
- 1 tbsp milk of choice

Instructions

1. Combine all your ingredients with a high-speed blender or any food processor accessible and blend it until you get a thick batter.
2. After blending, let your batter sit for about 5-10 minutes, thereby allowing the coconut flour to become thick. If the dough becomes too thick, supplement it with more milk or any liquid of your choice.
3. Grease a large non-stick pan and preheat it over low/medium heat. When the pan is hot, pour a one-quarter portion of the whole batter onto the hot pan and cover it immediately. Let it cook for about 2-3 minutes and flip when you see bubbles on the edges. Using the rest of the batter, repeat the process.
4. When the pancakes are ready, prepare your sticky cinnamon roll glaze. Dissolve the coconut butter and add cinnamon to it. Thin out some milk and drizzle it over the top of the pancake. Enjoy!

Nutrition Facts

Serves: 1serving / Calories: 125kcal / Carbohydrates: 3.5g / Protein: 7g / Fat: 7g

LOW CARB CINNAMON ROLL MUFFINS

This super fluffy and bakery-style muffins recipe is prepared using almond flour without any eggs and butter, but super moist. Dairy-Free, Sugar-Free, Grain-Free, Gluten-Free.

Ingredients

- 1 tsp baking powder
- 1/2 cup coconut oil
- 1/2 cup almond flour
- 1 tbsp cinnamon
- 1/2 cup pumpkin puree (Alternatively unsweetened applesauce, mashed banana or mashed cooked sweet potato)
- 2 scoops vanilla protein powder (32-34 grams per scoop)
- 1/2 cup nut/seed butter of choice (you can use almond butter, peanut butter, sunflower seed butter, etc.)

For the glaze

- 2 tsp lemon juice
- 1 tbsp granulated sweetener of choice
- 1/4 cup milk of choice
- 1/4 cup coconut butter

Instructions

1. Preheat your oven to about 350°F. Line the inside of your 12-count muffin tin with muffin liners

paper and set it aside. For this process you can also use a mini muffin tin.

2. Combine your dry and wet ingredients in a large mixing bowl and mix well it until fully incorporated.

3. Distribute the cinnamon roll muffin batter uniformly between the muffin liners. Allow it to bake for about 10-15 minutes then insert a skewer in the middle at precisely 10 minutes to see if the skewer comes out dry and clean. The muffins are cooked if the skewer comes out clean. Allow it to cool down in the pan for about 5 minutes before moving to it to the wire rack to cool down totally.

4. When the muffin is cooled, prepare your sticky cinnamon roll glaze by putting all ingredients together and mixing them. Sprinkle the cinnamon glaze over the muffin tops and allow it to firm up.

Nutrition Facts

Serves: 1 muffin / Calories: 112kcal / Carbohydrates: 3g / Protein: 5g / Fat: 9g

PEANUT BUTTER CHIA PUDDING

This recipe is a very healthy keto-veggie breakfast made with unsweetened almond milk, sugar-free monk fruit syrup, and chia seeds.

Ingredients

- 1 cup peanut butter (no added oil, no added sugar)
- 2-3 drops monk fruit pure extract
- 1 + 1/4 cup unsweetened Almond Milk
- 1 teaspoon vanilla essence
- 1 teaspoon dark chocolate chunks (sugar-free or 85% cocoa)
- 1/4 cup sugar-free maple-flavored syrup
- 1 teaspoon peanut butter
- 1/2 teaspoon crushed peanuts
- 1 teaspoon melted dark chocolate (sugar-free or 85% cocoa)
- 1/4 teaspoon sea salt
- 1/4 cup ground chia seeds (27g)

Instructions

1. Add every ingredient (no particular order needed) in a high-speed blender or any food processor-accessible.
2. Blend the ingredients for about 30 seconds then stop to scrape the sides of the blender with a

spatula. Continue mixing until you obtain a smooth and creamy mixture.

3. At this stage, I recommend checking the sweetness and adjusting for a sweeter pudding by using stevia drops or few extra drops of monk fruit extract. You can also make adjustments to flavor by using additional maple-flavored syrup, but the more syrup you add, the more liquid the puddling will be. That's why adjusting flavor with drops is the most preferred.

4. Transfer the pudding into six small glass jars and then refrigerate it for at least 3 hours to get the best creamy flavors and texture.

5. Serve it with your preferred toppings. I suggest a drizzle of melted sugar-free chocolate, sugar-free dark chocolate chunks, a pinch of crushed peanuts or a drizzle of peanut butter.

6. For conservation, store in the freezer for not more than five days in an airtight container. Serve and enjoy for breakfast.

Nutrition Facts

Serves: 1 Pudding / Calories 295kcal / Fat 24g / Carbohydrates 15.8g / Protein 10.6g

SUPER EGGY VEGAN TOFU SCRAMBLE

This recipe is high in protein and is super eggy vegan tofu scramble, as they are known. This rich and satisfying vegan breakfast comes close to scrambled eggs without being scrammed eggs, and that is pretty cool. Suitable for vegans who are missing eggs and who only want a sumptuous, healthy breakfast.

Ingredients

- 1/2 tsp Garlic Powder
- 8oz (220g) Extra Firm Tofu
- 2 Tbsp. Nutritional Yeast
- 1 Tbsp Vegan Butter
- 1/2 tsp Turmeric
- 1/4 tsp Onion Powder
- 1/3 cup (80ml) Soy Milk
- 1/2 tsp Paprika
- 1 tsp Dijon Mustard
- 1/4 tsp Black Salt

For Serving:

- Sliced Avocado
- Chopped Chives
- Fried Tomatoes
- Black Pepper

Instructions

1. Using a fork, mash the tofu and make sure to keep a few large chunks.
2. In a jar, combine the nutritional turmeric, yeast, powdered garlic, onion, dijon mustard, black salt,

and peppers. Introduce the soy milk and whisk it so that you have a beautifully mixed sauce.

3. Fill the frying pan with the vegan butter and heat until hot. Add the tofu into the pan and fry until slightly browned, do it carefully to avoid breaking it too much when moving it around in the saucepan.

4. Introduce the sauce and fold the tofu. Fry it until the intended consistency has been attained; the tofu will absorbe the sauce so you can choose to have it wet or dry.

5. Add black pepper and chopped chives to the top and serve with sliced avocados and fried tomatoes.

Nutrition Facts

Serves: 1/2 the Recipe / Calories: 206Kcal / Fat: 13.1g / Carbohydrates: 3.8g / Protein: 20.3g

STRAWBERRY COCONUT CHIA PUDDING

It takes only five ingredients and 10 minutes to prepare this delightful Strawberry Coconut Chia Pudding. Your new vegan breakfast favorite!

Ingredients

- 1 cup almond milk
- 1 ts vanilla extract
- 3 tbs chia seeds
- 1 can full-fat coconut milk, refrigerated

Strawberry Jam:

- 1 ts coconut sugar
- 1 cup strawberries, frozen

Toppings:

- Berries, fresh or frozen
- 1 ts strawberry jam

Optional:

- Quinoa puffs
- 1 ts almond butter
- Passion fruit

Instructions

1. In a container/jar, mix chia seeds, milk, and vanilla. Blend it together and put it in the refrigerator overnight.
2. Take it out of the fridge in the morning.

3. Prepare your strawberry jam: put the dried strawberries and shea oil in a pot and boil for about 15 minutes at low temperature. Allow the strawberries to dissolve and cook down. Then mix the jam smoothly with an immersion blender and cook for a few minutes until it grows thick. Any remaining jam you can store for up to a week in the fridge.
4. Open a cocoa milk can and scoop off the solid cream. Save cocoa water leftover for smoothies or drinking. Stir in coconut milk or coconut water if your chia pudding is too thick.
5. Whisk or stir the thick coconut cream together.
6. Arrange your pudding in glass or jar in layers: begin with a strawberry jam layer, add a chia pudding layer and cover with coconut milk layer. Repeat until every ingredient is used up.
7. Top with some fresh or frozen strawberry jam and berries.
8. Add an almond cheese teaspoon, some quinoa puffs, and passion fruits, as an option. Serve and enjoy!

Nutrition Facts

Serves: 266 Grams / Calories: 264Kcal / Fat: 21.5g / Carbohydrates: 11.8g / Protein: 3.8g

LOW CARB VEGAN PANCAKES

These low carb gluten-free, vegan pancakes provide the ideal breakfast for a lovely and relaxed weekend. They are free of dairy products, egg, soy and sugar and likewise high in protein and omega-3 fatty and fiber. This is the keto pancake!

Ingredients

- Liquid stevia or Swerve to taste
- 1/4 cup unsweetened almond milk
- 2 tbsp unsweetened almond butter
- Pinch of salt (only if you are not using salted almond butter)
- 1 tbsp coconut flour
- 1/2 tsp baking powder
- 1 tbsp ground flax

Instructions

1. Heat the frying pan to use at medium/low heat. Oil the pot lightly with your choice of oil and bear in mind to count it towards the nutrition information.
2. Mix the almond milk and almond butter in a small dish.
3. Combine the dry ingredients in another dish until mixed well.
4. Mix wet ingredients together with dry ones and mash-up until thoroughly mixed. Allow it to rest

for about 3-5 minutes so that the fluid can be absorbed by the flax and coconut flour.

5. Slather the batter on your saucepan and slowly spread into pancakes. If the mixture is hard to distribute, wet a spoon and use it as spatula; cook for approximately 4-5 minutes until the pancakes easily flipped. Check at precisely 3 minutes by softly putting your spatula under the pancake.

6. You want to watch these small bubbles all over the area, just like regular pancakes. If golden underneath, flip it and let it cook for another 2-3 pancakes until adequately cooked.

7. Top the pancake with sugar-free syrup, coconut cream, berries, vegan butter, berries, or more almond butter (or any combo of these foods) and enjoy!

Nutrition Facts

Serves: 1 full recipe / Calories: 259.6kcal /
Carbohydrates: 13.9g / Protein: 9.6g / Fat: 20.8g

VEGETARIAN KETO CLUB SALAD

Yes, this breakfast meal is very different from typical club sandwiches or even club salads, but the taste will have you cheerfully munching on the vegetables without even longing for meat and bread!

Ingredients

- 1/2 teaspoon garlic powder
- 2 tablespoons sour cream
- 3 cups romaine lettuce, torn into pieces
- 1 tablespoon dijon mustard
- 1 tablespoon milk
- 1 teaspoon dried parsley
- 3 large hard-boiled eggs, sliced
- 1/2 teaspoon onion powder
- 4 ounces cheddar cheese, cubed
- 1/2cup cherry tomatoes (halved)
- 2 tablespoons mayonnaise
- 1 cup diced cucumber

Instructions

1. Combine and mix the mayonnaise, sour cream, and dried herb together to prepare the dressing.
2. Add a tablespoon of milk and blend. Add another tablespoon of milk when the dressing seems too thick. If you do more milk, don't forget to add it to the final protein/fat/carb count!

3. Lay the fresh vegetables, cheese, and sliced egg in your salad. Fill the center with a spoonful of Dijon mustard.
4. Glaze with prepared dressing, approximately 2 tablespoons per serving then toss to coat.

Nutrition Facts

Serves: 3 servings / Calories 329.67Kcal / Fat 26.32 g / Carbs 4.83 g / Protein 16.82 g

FRESH BELL PEPPER BASIL PIZZA

We will be making a completely fresh and delicious pizza. Topped with yellow and red bell pepper, this provides every bite with a great crunch, sweetness and new look.

Ingredients

Pizza Base

- 2 tablespoons cream cheese
- 1/2 teaspoon salt
- 1/2 teaspoon pepper
- 2 tablespoons psyllium husk
- 1 large egg

- 2 tablespoons fresh Parmesan cheese
- 1/2 cup almond flour
- 6 ounces mozzarella cheese
- 1 teaspoon Italian seasoning

Toppings

- 1/4 cup Rao's Marinara Sauce
- 4 ounces shredded cheddar cheese

- 1 medium vine tomato
- 2-3 tablespoons fresh chopped basil
- 2-3 medium bell pepper

Instruction

1. Preheat the oven to use to about 400°F.
2. The mozzarella cheese should be microwaved for 40-50 seconds or until fully melted and flexed.

3. Mix your cheese with the remainder of your pizza ingredients (except for toppings) and use your hand to mix together.
4. Flatten the dough and make a circle with your hands or a rolling pin.
5. Bake and remove pizza from the oven after 10 minutes. Put the toppings on top of the pizza and bake for extra 8-10 minutes.
6. Remove the pizza from the oven and leave to cool.

Nutrition Facts

Servings: 2 pizzas / Calories 411.5Kcal / Fats 31.32g / Carbs 6.46g / Protein 22.26g.

BREAKFAST BROWNIE MUFFINS

The meal is an easy grab-and-go type of breakfast and extremely straightforward to prepare. You can always make your own low carb maple syrup to add to the batter, if you do not wish to use an already made one.

Ingredients

- 1 cup golden flaxseed meal
- 2 tablespoons coconut oil
- 1 teaspoon apple cider vinegar
- 1/2 tablespoon baking powder
- 1 tablespoon cinnamon
- 1/2 teaspoon salt
- 1 large egg
- 1 teaspoon vanilla extract
- 1/4 cup slivered almonds
- 1/2 cup pumpkin puree
- 1/4 cup sugar-free caramel syrup
- 1/4 cup cocoa powder

Instructions

1. Preheat the oven to use to 350°F and mix all ingredients together in a deep mixing bowl.
2. Line the inside part of the muffin tin with paper liners and pour approximately 1/4 tablespoon of batter into each liner.
3. Spread the slivered almonds over the top of every muffin and press them softly to stick.

4. Bake it for 15 minutes (approximately) in the oven. You ought to see the muffins rise and set at the top.

Nutrition Facts

Serves: 6 servings / Calories 193 / Fats 14.09g / Carbs 4.37g / Protein 6.98g

CHARRED VEGGIE AND FRIED GOAT CHEESE SALAD

If you are looking for something warm and hearty, but that still brings you that crunch that you want from veggies, this is the dish for you!

Ingredients

- 4 ounces of goat cheese, cut in pieces (4 thick medallions)
- 2 tablespoons sesame seeds
- 1 teaspoon garlic flakes
- 1 teaspoon onion flakes
- 1/2 cup sliced baby portobello mushrooms
- 1 medium red bell pepper (cut in 8 pieces, seeds removed)
- 2 tablespoons poppy seeds
- 4 cups arugula, divided between two bowls
- 1 tablespoon avocado oil

Instructions

1. On a tiny plate, combine the sesame seeds, poppy, onion and garlic flakes.
2. Coat on both ends each piece of goat cheese. Put it on a plate and then into the fridge until the cheese is ready for frying.
3. Prepare a nonstick spray skillet and heat moderately. On both sides, char the peppers and mushrooms until the pieces darken and the

pepper becomes soft. Add it into the bowls of arugula.

4. In the skillet, put the cold goat cheese and fry it for about 30 seconds on either side. It melts very rapidly, so be careful as you flip every piece!

5. Fill the salad with the cheese and drizzle it with the avocado oil. Serve warm and enjoy!

Nutrition Facts

Serves: 2 servings / Calories 350Kcal / Fat 27.61 g / Carbs 7.08 g / Protein 16.09 g

CRISPY TOFU AND BOK CHOY SALAD

Baked tofu is lovely. You'll get a rich and flavorful little cube with crunchy outsides instead of the gooey, smooth and flavorless pile that people commonly portray.

Ingredients

Oven-Baked Tofu

- 1 tablespoon soy sauce
- 1 tablespoon water
- 2 teaspoons minced garlic
- 15 ounces extra-firm tofu
- 1 tablespoon rice wine vinegar
- Juice 1/2 lemon
- 1 tablespoon sesame oil

Bok Choy Salad

- 1 tablespoon peanut butter
- 2 tablespoons soy sauce
- 7 drops liquid stevia
- 1 stalk green onion
- 2 tablespoons chopped cilantro
- Juice 1/2 lime
- 9 ounces bok choy
- 3 tablespoons coconut oil
- 1 tablespoon sambal Olek

Instructions

1. Press the tofu dry for approximately 5-6 hours.
2. Mix together all the marinade components (garlic, soy, vinegar, sesame oil, lemon, and water).
3. Have the tofu chopped into squares and put it together with the marinade in a plastic bag. Let it marinate overnight (if it is not possible at least 30 minutes).
4. Preheat the oven to about 350°F. On a baking sheet lined with greaseproof paper, place tofu and bake for 30-35 minutes.
5. Combine all the salad dressing ingredients in a mixing bowl (excluding bok choy). Then add spring onion and cilantro.
6. Chop the bok choy, like you would cut cabbage, into tiny pieces.
7. Take tofu off the oven, and put the tofu, bok choy, and sauce in your salad. Serve and enjoy!

Nutrition Facts

Serves: 3 servings / Calories 398.59Kcal / Fats 30.43g / Carbs 6.68g / Protein 24.11g

VEGAN SESAME TOFU AND EGGPLANT

Bear in mind if you have never before cooked tofu, that the firmness of tofu is essential to the recipe.

Ingredients

- 1 tablespoon olive oil
- 1 teaspoon crushed red pepper flakes
- 1/4 cup sesame seeds
- 1 pound block firm tofu
- Salt and pepper to taste
- 2 teaspoons Swerve confectioners
- 3 tablespoons rice vinegar
- 1 cup chopped cilantro
- 1 whole eggplant
- 4 tablespoons toasted sesame oil
- 1/4 cup soy sauce
- 2 cloves garlic, finely minced

Instructions

1. Preheat the pan to use to approximately 200°F. Start by removing the tofu block from its branding and wrap it with towels on paper. Put a big plate above it to weigh it down. You can use a large tin of vegetables or anything convenient. Allow the tofu to sit for some time to push out some water.
2. Combine in a full mixing bowl approximately 3 tablespoons rice vinegar, minced garlic, 1/4 cup of

cilantro, crushed red pepper flakes and 2 cubes of toasted sesame sauce. Whisk it together.

3. After you have peeled the eggplant, cut it int thin and long strips. You can either julienne roughly using your hand or by using a julienne attachment with a mandolin to give a more accurate "noodles." The eggplant may also be mixed with marinade.

4. Under medium-low heat, introduce a tablespoon of olive oil to a skillet. Cook the eggplants until they are soft. The eggplant will take up all the liquids, so you can add some more olive or sesame oil if you have any problems with it sticking to the pan. Just make sure you adjust your tracking of the nutrition count.

5. Switch off your oven. Put the remaining cilantro in the eggplant and place the noodles in a safe dish tray. Utilize the oven, by putting the dish in, to keep it warm, and remember to cover it with a foil or lid Clean up the skillet and heat it up again on the stovetop.

6. Slice the Tofu into eight pieces. Distribute the seeds of sesame on a plate. Press each tofu to the seeds on both sides.

7. Add approximately two tablespoons of sésame oil to the skillet. Fry the tofu on both sides for 5 minutes or until they start crisping. Add 1/4 cup of soy sauce in the pan and coat the tofu. Cook until the pieces of tofu appear browned and caramelized.

8. Get the noodles out of the oven and stack the tofu on top.

Nutrition Facts

Serves: 4 servings / Calories 292.75Kcal / Fats 24.45g / Carbs 6.87g / Protein 11.21g

LOW CARB FRIED MAC & CHEESE

A new version of the classic Mac&Cheese! Healthier, easy&quick, low carb, and delicious!

Ingredients

- 3/4 teaspoon rosemary
- 1 medium cauliflower, riced
- 2 teaspoons paprika
- 3 large eggs
- 1 + 1/2 cups shredded cheddar cheese
- 1 teaspoon turmeric

Instructions

1. Use any available food processor to rice the Cauliflower.
2. Cook for five minutes in the microwave.
3. Wriggle it in a kitchen or paper towels to dry it out. You want the lowest possible moisture.
4. Add your eggs, cheese, and spices and blend together (do it one at a time, you don't want to have a watery blend).
5. At high temperatures, heat the saucepan and add olive oil and coconut oil.
6. Out of the cauliflower blend, make out small patties.
7. Fry until crisp on both sides.

Nutrition Facts

Serves: Per Fried Mac & Cheese Patty /
Calories 39.67Kcal / Fats 2.71g / Carbs 0.96g /
Protein 2.59g

GRILLED CHEESE SANDWICH

Most people are attracted to the simpleness of grilled cheese. Warm, melty, cheese with gooey, spewing the side of the toasted and crunchy bread.

Ingredients

Bun Ingredients

- 2 tablespoons soft butter
- 1 + 1/2 tablespoons psyllium husk powder
- 1/2 teaspoon baking powder
- 2 large eggs
- 2 tablespoons almond flour

Fillings & Extras

- 1 tablespoons butter
- 2 ounces cheddar cheese

Instructions

1. In a container, blend all bun ingredients. Continue to mix until it thickens.
2. In a square pan or container, add the mixture and then level it up. If necessary, clean the sides.
3. For 90 seconds, microwave and check whether it's done. Otherwise, proceed to 15 seconds increments.
4. Remove the container break and slice in half once cooked.

5. Put the cheese in the bun, heat butter over medium heat, and fry the grilled cheese until you are satisfied with the texture.

Nutrition Facts

Serves: 1 serving / Calories 803Kcal / 69.95g Fats / Carbs 6.14g / Protein 25.84g

VEGETARIAN GREEK COLLARD WRAPS

This inspired Greek veggie wrap is filled with square veggies and thick hunks of salty feta, complemented by the creamy tang of tzatziki. Tzatziki is a simple spread of garlic, greek yogourt, lemon, and grated cucumber.

Ingredients

- 2 tablespoons olive oil
- 1 tablespoon white vinegar
- Salt and pepper to taste
- 2 tablespoons minced fresh dill
- 2.5 ounces (1/4 of a whole) cucumber, seeded and grated
- 1 cup full-fat plain Greek yogurt
- 1 teaspoon garlic powder
- Tzatziki Sauce

The Wrap

- 1/2 medium red bell pepper, julienned
- 1/2 block (4-oz) feta, cut into 4 (1-inch thick) strips
- 8 kalamata olives, halved
- 4 cherry tomatoes, halved
- 1/2 cup purple onion, diced
- 4 large collard green leaves, washed
- 1 medium cucumber, julienned

Instructions

1. Mix all tzatziki sauce ingredients together and keep the rest in the refrigerator. After you have grated the cucumber, squeeze out all the water from it.
2. Begin preparing the collard green wraps by cleaning the leaves, and trimming each sheet from the fibrous stem.
3. Add 2 tablespoons tzatziki in the middle of each wrap and spread out the sauce.
4. Lay the feta, olives, pepper, cucumber, and tomato in the center of the wrap. Imagine they are being piled up on top of each other rather than spread out!
5. Fold like a burrito, bending in the middle on each side and folding the rounded end across the filling and roll.
6. Slice in half and serve in plastic for a quick breakfast with any remaining tzatziki or wrap!

Nutrition Facts

Serves: 4 wraps, 1 per serving / Calories 165.34Kcal / Fat 11.25 g / Carbs 7.36g / Protein 6.98g

SUN-DRIED TOMATO PESTO MUG CAKE

Fresh, tasty, and unique. These words are the perfect definition of this cake. Tomato is fantastic and can add a unique sense of flavor, moisture, and taste to your dish.

Ingredients

Base

- 2 tablespoons almond flour
- 2 tablespoons butter
- 1 large egg
- 1/2 teaspoon baking powder

Flavor

- Pinch salt
- 5 teaspoons sun-dried tomato pesto
- 1 tablespoon almond flour

Instructions

1. Combine all of the ingredients and mix.
2. Microwave the mixture for 75 seconds at a high temperature.
3. Slam cup lightly against any plate available to take out the mug cake. Add additional tomato pesto, then serve!

Nutrition Facts

Serves: 1 serving / Calories 429Kcal / Fats 40.45g /
Carbs 5.32g / Protein 12.34g

LEMON RASPBERRY SWEET ROLLS

These rolls are tasteful so much that nobody guesses that they are Keto. The dough, like regular pastry dough, is puffy and sensitive.

Ingredients

For the lemon cream cheese filling:

- 1/2 tsp. vanilla extract
- 1 tsp. lemon juice
- Zest from one lemon (about 2 teaspoons)
- 2 tbsp. stevia erythritol blend
- 2 tbsp. butter, room temperature
- 4 oz. cream cheese, room temperature
- 1 tsp. lemon extract

For the raspberry sauce:

- 2 teaspoons lemon juice
- 1/2 cup frozen raspberries
- 1/4 teaspoon xanthan gum
- 2 tablespoons stevia erythritol blend
- 1 tablespoon water

For the dough:

- 1 large egg
- 1 teaspoon vanilla extract
- 1/4 cup stevia erythritol blend

- 1 cup superfine almond flour
- 1 + 1/4 teaspoons baking powder
- 2 cups part-skim mozzarella cheese

1/4 teaspoon xanthan gum

For the lemon glaze: (optional)

- 1 teaspoon lemon juice
- 1 + 1/2 tablespoons unsweetened almond milk, at room temperature
- 2 tablespoons stevia erythritol blend
- 1/2 ounce cream cheese, room temperature
- 1/4 teaspoon vanilla extract
- 2 tablespoons butter, room temperature
- 1/4 teaspoon lemon extract

Instructions

Lemon Cream Cheese Filling:

1. Place the cream cheese, lemon zest, ginger extract, citrus peel, butter, sweetener and lemon juice on an electric mixer and blend until soft. Set it aside.

Raspberry Sauce:

1. Whip sweetener and xanthan gum in a medium saucepan. Continue to add water and lemon juice slowly while you whip.
2. Set the heating source to medium-low. Stir

continuously while adding frozen raspberries. Remove the sauce from the heat when it starts to simmer and set aside.

Dough:

1. Preheat the oven to use to about 350°F. Sprinkle the pan with some coconut oil or butter. Have a convenient rolling pin and two 15 inch sheet of parchment.
2. Have a double boiler ready. A medium bowl with a medium saucepan that would sit well on the double boiler is perfect for this purpose. In the saucepan or lower part of the double boiler, put approximately 2 inches of water. Set over high temperature and uncover it to a simmer. Reduce heat to low once simmering.
3. Meanwhile, mix stevia or erythritol sweetener, xanthan gum, almond flour, and baking powder using whisks in the upper part of the double boiler (make sure it is not over the water).
4. Add in the vanilla extract and egg. The mixture is going to be very thick.
5. Add the mozzarella cheese to the mixture and place the bowl over the simmering water. Protect your fingers from the hot bowl and the steam that escapes from the pot. For this intent, a silicone mitten operates well.
6. Constantly stir the mixture as the cheese continues to melt and combine with the flour. It's going to start to look like bread dough.

7. Once the cheese is fully melted, move the dough to a ready parchment piece. Knead the dough a number of occasions to merge the cheese and the flour mixture entirely. Knead dough into the rectangular form and cover with the second parchment piece. Roll out dough in a rectangle of approximately 12 X 15. Remove the top parchment.
8. Spread the lemon cream cheese filling on the dough evenly and leave approximately one and a half-inch on the edges uncovered. Lay the mixture of the raspberry sauce over the lemon cream cheese filling.
9. Roll the dough into a log form starting on the lengthy side. To seal out, press the long outer edge.
10. Cut the log crosswise in 8 different parts with a serrated knife. Assemble the rolls in a ready pot in such a way that one stays in the center, and the rest are circled around the middle one.
11. Bake until golden brown for 24-26 minutes.

Lemon glaze:

1. Using a small bowl, whip cream cheese and butter with an electric mixer until smooth.
2. Then add lemon juice, lemon extract vanilla, and sweetener and blend until incorporated.
3. Slowly introduce the almond milk, a teaspoon at a time, and beating the mixture between each addition.

Nutrition Facts

Serves: 8 servings / Calories 272.25Kcal / Fats 23.18g /
Carbs 5.24g / Protein 10.04g

VEGAN KETO PORRIDGE

This vegan keto porridge breakfast recipe holds you full throughout the morning. Apply your favorite toppings into this creamy and thick breakfast option to personalize the flavor.

Ingredients

- 3 tablespoons golden flaxseed meal
- 2 tablespoons vegan vanilla protein powder
- Powdered erythritol to taste
- 2 tablespoons coconut flour
- 1 + 1/2 cups unsweetened almond milk

Instructions

1. Combine the golden flaxseed, coconut flour, and protein powder in a mixing bowl and mix the ingredients together.
2. Into the saucepan, along with almond milk, add the mixture, then cook over medium temperature. At first, it's going to seem very loose.
3. You could add your favorite quantity of sweetener when it thickens. Serve with the toppings you like and enjoy!

Nutrition Facts

Serving: 1 serving / Calories 249Kcal / Fats 13.07g / Carbs 5.78g / Protein 17.82g

ULTIMATE KETO COFFEE CAKE

It is not common that I call a recipe "the supreme" version, but this one hits the nail on the head. It is ideal in all ways, blended with a smooth texture and exquisite tastes.

Ingredients

Base

- 1/4 tsp. Liquid Stevia
- 1/4 cup Erythritol
- 6 Eggs, Separated
- 1/4 Cup Unflavored Protein Powder
- 1/4 tsp. Cream of Tartar
- 2 tsp. Vanilla Extract
- 6 Oz. Cream Cheese

Filling

- 1/4 Cup Maple Syrup Substitute
- 1 Tbsp. Cinnamon
- 1 1/2 Cup Almond Flour
- 1/4 cup Erythritol
- 1/2 Stick Butter

Instructions

1. Preheat the oven to use to about 325°F. Then isolate the eggs from egg whites.
2. Start by creaming erythritol with egg yolks, then add all the other ingredients, except for tartar and egg whites and whisk together.

3. Whip the tartar cream and egg whites until stiff peaks are formed.
4. Tuck one half of the white egg into the yolks and then the other half in the mixture. Be comparatively mild to keep the egg whites airy.
5. Combine all the filling ingredients to form a dough. Then mix together.
6. In dark metal cake pan, put the base batter and top it with half the cinnamon filling. If it doesn't fall by itself, push it down.
7. Bake for 20 minutes, then add the remainder of the filling dough to your cake as toppings.
8. Bake for extra 20-30 minutes or until the toothpick comes out dry and clean. Allow 10–20 minutes to cool before the pan is removed.

Nutrition Facts

Serves: 8 slices / Calories 320.75Kcal / Fats 28.01g / Carbs 4.24g / Protein 12.85g

ROASTED MUSHROOM AND WALNUT CAULIFLOWER GRITS

The handling of the cauliflower is the key to this delicacy. Cold processing of the florets and steaming them in the pot with some water is essential.

Ingredients

- 3 cloves garlic, minced
- 6 ounces baby portobello mushrooms, sliced
- 2 tablespoons olive oil
- 1 medium cauliflower
- 1 cup shredded sharp cheddar
- 1/2 cup chopped walnuts
- Salt to taste
- 1/2 cup water
- 1 tablespoon smoked paprika
- 1 tablespoon rosemary
- 2 tablespoons butter

Instructions

1. Thoroughly heat the oven to 400°F and place a foil on the cookie sheet. Combine in a small dish the walnuts, minced garlic, rosemary, sliced mushrooms, and smoked paprika and sprinkle some olive oil. Season it with some salt and toss it to coat.
2. Distribute the mixture uniformly on the cookie sheet and fry for 15 minutes in the oven.
3. Process one head of cauliflower florets by pulsing very nicely in a meal processor.

4. Steam the prepared cauliflower in a pot and cover it with a half cup of water for around 5 minutes or till the mixture is tender. You wouldn't want it to be too soft, because it'll have to look like grits.

5. Pour half into the cauliflower grits and stir it, leave it for 3 minutes on medium-low heat to simmer. This is the best moment to get the milk heated.

6. Combine the butter and sharp cheddar, then reduce heat to low until the mixture is well combined and creamy. Season it with some salt to give it flavor. Add another one-quarter cup of water if you like your grits runny.

7. Take the roasting pot off the oven once you have soft mushrooms and a deep brown edge.

8. Serve cauliflower grits hot and top it with some mushroom sauce and extra butter if you like!

Nutrition Facts

Servings: 4 servings / Calories 455Kcal / Fats 36.5g / Carbs 11.28g / Protein 15.28g

RED COCONUT CURRY

Let yourself be able to add more vegetables or tofu and make it safer and ready to become a breakfast recipe.

Ingredients

- 1 teaspoon minced ginger
- 4 tablespoons coconut oil
- 1/2 cup coconut cream (alternatively coconut milk)
- 1 tablespoon red curry paste
- 1/4 medium onion
- 2 teaspoons soy sauce
- 1 cup broccoli florets
- 1 teaspoon minced garlic
- 2 teaspoons Fysh sauce
- 1 large handful of spinach

Instructions

1. Chop hairy garlic and tomatoes. Add 2 tablespoons of Coconut oil in a saucepan and heat to medium.
2. Add some onions to the pan once hot, then cook until it is semi-translucent. Add some garlic into the pan to make the mixture brown.
3. Turn temperature to medium-low and add some broccoli. Turn everything together really well.

4. After the broccoli is baked in part, transfer vegetables to the bottom of the oven and add curry sauce. Allow it to cook for approximately 45-60 seconds.
5. Add some spinach as topping on the broccoli spinach and once it starts wilting, add the coconut cream and the remaining cocoa oil.
6. Add the soy, Fysh sauce and ginger and stir together. Let it cool, relying on the density you need, for 5-10 minutes.

Nutrition Facts

Servings: 2 servings / Calories 398Kcal / Fats 40.73g / Carbs 7.86g / Protein 3.91g

THREE CHEESE QUICHE STUFFED PEPPERS

This cheesy quiche stuffed pepper is an easy and more comfortable breakfast. The mixture of mozzarella, full-fat ricotta, and shredded parmesan is used in the making of this fluffy, lightly seasoned egg filling.

Ingredients

- 1/2 cup grated Parmesan cheese
- 1/4 teaspoon dried parsley
- 1/2 cup ricotta cheese
- 1 teaspoon garlic powder
- 2 tablespoons Parmesan cheese, to garnish
- 2 medium bell peppers (seeds removed and sliced in half)
- 4 large eggs
- 1/2 cup shredded mozzarella
- 1/4 cup baby spinach leaves

Instructions

1. Heat the oven to use to about 375°F. Prepare and cut the peppers into four equal half and remove the seeds.
2. Mix the three kinds of cheese, garlic powder, eggs and parsley in a small food processor.
3. In each pepper, pour the egg mixture, and fill it below the cap. Place a couple of spinach leaves at

the top of the mix and push them under the egg with a fork. Cover with a foil and bake for about 35-45 minutes or just leave it until the egg is cooked correctly.

4. Slather some Parmesan cheese and cook for an additional three to five minutes or leave until the top begins to get brown.

Nutrition Facts

Serves: 4 servings / Calories 245.5Kcal / Fat 16.28g / Carbs 5.97g / Protein 17.84g

CAULIFLOWER MAC & CHEESE

This mac and cheese recipe with cauliflower is spicy, cheesy and brightly colored. The shiny yellow color comes from turmeric. The sauce has a blend of mustard and garlic flavors, but cheddar cheese is the star.

Ingredients

- 8 ounces cheddar cheese, shredded
- 1 teaspoon turmeric
- 1 teaspoon Dijon mustard
- 1/2 teaspoon powdered garlic
- 1 cup heavy whipping cream
- 4 ounces cream cheese, cubed
- Salt and pepper to taste
- 2 pounds frozen cauliflower florets

Instructions

1. Prepare the cauliflower florets following the instructions of the package.
2. Allow the cream to simmer. Stir the cream cheese with a whisk and continue to mix until smooth.
3. Stir the shredded Cheddar cheese in 6 ounces. Save the remaining 2 ounces for later use. Continue to mix until the cheese completely melts into the sauce.
4. Incorporate some turmeric, powdered garlic,

mustard Dijon, pepper and salt. The sauce turns into a smooth yellow color.

5. Ensure the cauliflower is properly drained then add it to the cheese sauce. Coat the florets equally with sauce.

6. Slather the remaining 2 ounces of cheddar cheese and continue to stir until all has melted.

Nutrition Facts

Serves: 8 servings / Calories 295.5Kcal / Fats 25.38g / Carbs 5.47g / Protein 10.63g

WARM ASIAN BROCCOLI SALAD

This recipe is the perfect breakfast dish for Asian barbecue keto small ribs or Korean BBQ bell peppers stuffed.

Ingredients

- 1 teaspoon fresh ginger, grated
- 2 tablespoons coconut oil
- Cilantro, as an optional garnish
- 1/2 teaspoon salt
- 1 tablespoon coconut aminos
- 1/4 teaspoon pepper
- 1/2 cup full-fat plain goat milk yogurt
- 1/2 tablespoon sesame seeds
- 12-ounce bag broccoli slaw

Instructions

1. In a big saucepan, preheat coconut oil over moderately high heat. Put the broccoli slaw in the saucepan and cover it. Let it cook for about 7 minutes.
2. Uncover and add pepper, salt, coconut aminos, and ginger. Take your skillet away from the heat, then add yogurt and sprinkle with sesame seeds.
3. If needed, garnish with cilantro.

Nutrition Facts

Serves: 8 servings / Calories 62Kcak / Fats 4.28g /
Carbs 3.62g / Protein 1.8g

LOW CARB BROCCOLI AND CHEESE FRITTERS

The broccoli fritters are not in any way similar to the everyday deep fried broccoli. These ones are crunchy and have a body to them. They are like hushpuppies, but instead of cornmeal, they are produced from broccoli.

Ingredients

The Fritters

- 2 large eggs
- 4 ounces mozzarella cheese
- 2 teaspoons baking powder
- 3/4 cup almond flour
- 4 ounces fresh broccoli
- Salt and pepper to taste
- 1/4 cup + 3 tablespoons flaxseed meal

The Sauce

- Salt and pepper to taste
- 1/4 cup mayonnaise
- 1/2 tablespoon lemon juice
- 1/4 cup fresh chopped dill

Instructions

1. Fill a food processor with broccoli and grind until

the broccoli is totally crushed.

2. Add 1/4 cup flaxseed meal, cheese, baking powder, and almond flour to the crushed broccoli and mix all together. Do it at this stage if you want to add additional seasonings (pepper and salt).
3. Add the eggs and blend well until all comes together.
4. Use your hand to roll the batter into balls, then use 3 tablespoons of flaxseed meal to coat the balls.
5. Use your hand to roll the batter into balls, then use 3 tablespoons of flaxseed meal to coat the balls.
6. Heat up your thick frying pan to about 375°F, lay fritters in the pan without overcrowding it.
7. Fry the fritters for around 3-5 minutes until golden brown. Once completed, place them on paper towels to dry out surplus grease and season them to your liking.
8. Make a dip with mayonnaise lemon and zesty dill. Serve and enjoy!

Nutrition Facts

Serves: 16 servings / Calories 103.9Kcal / Fats 8.35g / Carbs 1.89g / Protein 4.57g

CHEESY HEARTS OF PALM DIP

If you're tired and sick of ignoring hot and cheesy dips simply because you're susceptible to dairy, then this is for you! This recipe provides you the taste of crab by applying the low-carb vegetable hearts of the palm if you are toying with the thought of less meat or are already a dedicated vegetarian.

Ingredients

- 3 stalks green onions, chopped
- 1/2 cup Parmesan cheese, shredded
- 2 tablespoons Italian seasoning
- 1/4 cup Parmesan cheese, for topping
- 1 (14-ounce) can heart of palm, drained
- 2 large eggs (separate 1 of the eggs)
- 1/4 cup mayonnaise

Instructions

9. Heat your oven to about 350°F and make a small non-stick baking dish.
10. Mince your green onion bulbs and drain the heart of palm. It is not essential to pieces the palm before incorporating it to your food processor but can be helpful if you know an older or less stressful method.

11. Combine and mix the parmesan cheese, hearts of palm, mayo, onion, and seasoning in the food processor. Pulse until the combination is thoroughly sliced.
12. Fill the processor with a whole egg and an egg yolk. Pulse the combination 3 to 4 times.
13. Into the baking dish, pour the batter and leave it to cook for about 15-20 minutes or just leave it until it starts puffing up. Stir and add more Parmesan cheese to the mix as a topping.
14. Broil until the Parmesan cheese topping melts and starts to become brown. Serve hot and enjoy with keto crackers or veggies!

Nutrition Facts

Servings: 9 servings / Calories 116.25Kcal / Fat 9.15g / Carbs 2.87g / Protein 4.92g

VEGETARIAN KETO LUNCH RECIPES

Lunch is a tricky meal. It's not always possible to sit down and enjoy a tasty dish in everyday life. Of course, there are exceptions, like Sundays and holidays, but most of the time we need something quick, affordable and, possible, healthy. Here are some good low-carb recipes that can help you in busy situations but also in specials one.

VEGAN "FRENCH FRIES"

Well, now is the perfect time to know about this vegetable. Swede (also called Rutabaka) is a low-carb vegetable used as a substitute for potatoes in the keto meals.

Ingredients

- 1 large swede (washed, peeled & sliced into 1/4 spears)
- 1/2 teaspoon salt
- 1/2 teaspoon paprika
- Dash freshly ground black pepper
- 2 tablespoons coconut oil
- 1/4 teaspoon cloves, ground (if desired)

Instructions

1. Heat up the oven to use to about 450°F.
2. Swede spears should be transferred to a mixing bowl and dried with paper towels to help remove excess humidity.
3. In a small mixing bowl, combine paprika, ground cloves, salt, and coconut oil.
4. In a mixing bowl, pour the combination of coconut oil over the swede spears.
5. Place the oil-coated swede spear on an already prepared 2 parchment paper line of a baking sheet.

6. Place in a heated oven and bake for about 25-35 minutes until it is fried uniformly cooked.
7. Serve with vegan mayo or non-sugary ketchup.

Nutrition Facts

Serves: 4 servings / Calories 117 Kcal /
Carbs 9.6 grams / Protein 1.7 grams / Fat 7 grams

GARLIC MUSTARD BRUSSELS SPROUTS

These crispy garlic mustard Brussel sprouts with dijon sauce are the ideal weekend side dish or the perfect weekly snack!

Ingredients

- 1 tbsp minced garlic
- Ground black pepper
- 1 tbsp coconut aminos or homemade substitute
- 1/2 tbsp vegan Dijon mustard
- 1 garlic head, peeled & separated into cloves
- 1 lb. fresh Brussels sprouts, sliced in half lengthwise & retaining leaves that fall off
- 1 tbsp melted vegan butter

Instructions

1. Heat up the oven to use to about 400°F.
2. Prepare and line the big parchment paper with a baking sheet, then combine melted vegan butter, minced garlic, mustard, garlic cloves, coconut aminos, brussels sprouts and black pepper In a large mixing bowl.
3. Mix well until the sprouts are fully coated.
4. Set up the sprouts in a single layer on the prepared baking sheet.

5. Transfer the arranged sprouts into the preheated oven and grill for about 35-40 minutes.
6. Confirm if it's well seasoned and add additional pepper and salt if necessary.
7. Serve and enjoy!

Nutrition Facts

Serves: 4 servings / Calories: 242kcal / Carbohydrates: 22g / Protein: 9g / Fat: 15g

PORTOBELLO MUSHROOM WITH GUACAMOLE

The Portabello mushrooms are a perfect lunch meal baked with crushed spices and then drenched in guacamole. It's an appropriate appetizer!

Ingredients

- 3 tbsp (divided) olive oil
- 1 tsp onion powder
- 6 collard green leaves (rinsed with stems chopped off)
- 1/4 cup spicy or mild harissa
- 1 tsp cumin, ground
- 1 lb. portobello mushrooms (trim off stem, rinse and pat dry)

Guacamole Ingredients

- 2 tbsp red onion, chopped
- 1 + 1/2-2 tbsps lime or lemon juice
- Pinch of salt
- 2 ripe avocados, medium (halved and pitted)

Top With (If desired)

- 1 tbsp cilantro, chopped
- 2 tbsps tomatoes, chopped

Instructions

1. Combine 1 + 1/2 tablespoon of olive oil, harissa, onion powder and cumin in a large mixing bowl.

2. Stir thoroughly until properly combined.
3. Coat each mushroom evenly and entirely with the bowl mixture.
4. Let the mushroom marinate in the mixture for about 15 minutes.
5. Use a spoon or a fork to remove avocado flesh to a bowl.
6. To the avocado pan, add salt, cilantro, chopped tomatoes, lemon juice or lime and red onion.
7. Combine and mash until it is uniformly mixed and allow to sit.
8. Put the skillet or saute pan over medium-high heat and add 1 + 1/2 tablespoons of olive oil.
9. Fill in the heated oil with marinated mushrooms and boil for approximately 3 minutes.
10. Turn over the mushrooms and boil the other side for 2-3 minutes. It should be brown on each side.
11. Before slicing, place the mushrooms aside for 2-3 minutes to cool.
12. In each collard of green leaves, add coriander, cassava, chopped tomatoes, guacamole, and a few mushroom slices.
13. Serve and enjoy

Nutrition Facts

Serves: 1 serving / Fat 11.5g / Carbohydrates: 9.9g / Fiber: 6.1g / Protein: 3.5g

CAPRESE OMELET

Directly from the land of Mediterranea's diet, a tastefully and healthy recipe, adapted to keto but without losing any deliciousness. Mozzarella, tomato and basil, you can't go wrong with that!

Ingredients

- 6 eggs
- 2 tbsp olive oil
- 5 oz. sliced mozzarella cheese
- salt and pepper
- 1 tbsp olive oil
- 3 oz. tomatoes cut in slices

Instructions

1. In a mixing bowl, crack the eggs and add salt and pepper to your mixture.
2. Whisk until fully combined, then add basil and stir.
3. Pour the oil in a large pan, then heat it and fry the tomatoes for a few minutes.
4. Pour the mixture over the tomatoes. When the batter is firm add mozzarella cheese.
5. Low the heat and wait for the omelet to set. Serve and enjoy!

Nutrition Facts

Serves: 2 servings / Calories: 534 kcal / Carbohydrates: 4g / Protein: 33g/ Fat: 43g

OVEN-FRIED GREEN BEANS

Savor these delicious low carb gluten-free green beans alone or combine it with your favorite grilled meat (if you are not on a keto diet). It is baked with almond flour and Parmesan cheese

Ingredients

- Dash pepper
- 3 tbsp hot water + 1 tbsp flax meal (mixed separately)
- 1/4 cup parmesan cheese
- 1/2 tsp paprika
- 1 tsp garlic powder
- 2 tbsp olive oil + 1 tablespoon (for drizzling pan)
- 1 tsp kosher salt or sea salt
- 1 lb. fresh green beans
- 1/4 cup almond flour

Instructions

1. Heat up the oven to use to about 425°F.
2. Prepare 2 baking pans lined with aluminum foil.
3. Drizzle some olive oil into the prepared pan.
4. Rinse and trim the green beans.
5. Whisk flax meal and hot water together until a thick and well-combined mixture is produced.
6. In the flax meal combination, add green beans and mix until fully coated.
7. In another bowl, add the rest of the ingredients and blend until adequately combined.

8. Fill the coated green beans into the dry mixture and toss well.
9. Transfer the mixture of green beans into the baking pan and move them into the preheated oven.
10. Bake for around 15 minutes or until it's crisp.
11. Serve and enjoy.

Nutrition Facts

Servings: 6 servings / Calories: 145kcal / Carbohydrates: 7.6g / Protein: 5.2g / Fat: 11.6g

CREAMY VEGAN KETO MASH

This recipe utilizes cauliflower in its preparation, but other vegetables are ideal for the development of mash: rutabaga (swede), snowshoes, broccoli, and even asparagus.

Ingredients

- 1/2 cup vegan soured cream or cream cheese (if desired)
- 1 chopped white onion, small
- 2 chopped garlic cloves
- 1 large cauliflower (washed & sliced into smaller florets)
- Freshly ground black pepper
- 1/4 cup melted vegan butter + 4 tablespoons melted vegan butter (for topping)
- 1/2 teaspoon salt or more as necessary

Instructions

1. Heat the oven to use to approximately 450°F.
2. Fill the baking sheet with cauliflower florets and move to the preheated oven.
3. Allow it to bake for about 20 minutes or until properly cooked.
4. Over medium heat, add 2 tablespoons of melted vegan butter into a pan.
5. Stir some sliced onions and some garlic into the

oil and stir cook for about 5 minutes until mildly browned.

6. Pour the cooked cauliflower florets into a high-speed electric blender or any available food processor.

7. Incorporate two tbsp of melted vegan butter, pepper, salt, and the cooked onion mixture into the blender.

8. Blend the mixture until a smooth and creamy consistency is achieved. Serve and top up with more vegan butter.

Nutrition Facts

Servings: 4 servings / Carbs 7 grams /
Protein 3.7 grams / Fat 28 grams / Calories 302 kcal

VEGAN BUTTERED BRUSSELS SPROUTS

This is a guaranteed way to make Brussels sprouts that taste scrumptious, just perfect for the lunch and holiday season.

Ingredients

- Freshly ground black pepper, as needed
- 55g melted vegan butter
- 1/2 lemon, juiced
- 1.1g pounds Brussels sprouts (washed, halved or quartered)
- 1/2 teaspoon salt, as needed

Instructions

1. Heat the oven to use to about 400°F.
2. Introduce brussels sprouts into a large mixing bowl and judiciously cover it with lemon juice and melted butter.
3. Add some pepper and salt to add flavor.
4. Toss the sprouts until it's uniformly coated.
5. Move into the preheated oven and let it bake for about 25-35 minutes or until it is soft internally and crispy on the outside. Stir the mixture one or two times to be sure the sprouts are well-cooked.
6. Serve and enjoy.

Nutrition Facts

Servings: 4 servings / Carbs 6.8 grams /
Protein 4.2 grams / Fat 14.1 grams / Calories 180 kcal

LUNCH TOFU SCRAMBLE

This simple tofu scramble recipe is the vegan replacement for scrambled eggs. It is high in protein and requires only a few ingredients for its preparation.

Ingredients

- 1-2 tablespoons olive oil
- 1/2 (sliced thin) red pepper
- 1/4 (sliced thin) red onion
- 2 (chopped loosely) cups kale
- 8 oz. extra-firm tofu

Sauce Ingredients

- 1/2 teaspoon garlic powder
- 1/2 teaspoon sea salt
- 1/4 teaspoon turmeric, if desired
- Water, to thin
- 1/2 teaspoon cumin powder
- 1/4 teaspoon chili powder

Serve With (If desired)

- Salsa
- Fresh cilantro
- Hot Sauce

Instructions

1. Use an absorbent towel that is clean to wrap and pat dry the tofu.

2. Put a cast-iron skillet or any other flat and heavy kitchen appliance on top of the tofu for about 15 minutes to drain out the water.
3. Find a small mixing bowl and put all the sauce ingredients, excluding water.
4. Gradually add water to the sauce until it reaches the desired consistency, then allow it to sit.
5. Over medium heat, add about 1-2 tablespoons of olive oil into the skillet.
6. Introduce some onions and red pepper into the heated oil in the skillet.
7. Slather some salt and a pinch of pepper into the mixture of onion.
8. Then allow it to cook for about 5 minutes or until fully softened.
9. Put some kale into the skillet and add a little more salt and pepper into the pan mixture.
10. Put a lid on the skillet and let it steam for about 2 minutes.
11. Remove the tofu from the absorbent towel and use a fork to crush t into tiny bits.
12. Shift the veggies in the pot to one side of the skillet using a wooden spatula and position the tofu on the other side.
13. Stir-fry the veggies and tofu for additional 2 minutes before judiciously adding the sauce to the tofu and a little sauce over the vegetables.
14. Continue to stir the skillet mixture until the content is uniformly coated and combined.

15. Cook for approximately 5-7 minutes until tofu is brown.
16. Serve with hot sauce, fresh cilantro and/or salsa.

Nutrition Facts

Servings: 1/2 of the recipe / Fat: 4.7 g / Carbohydrates: 2.1 g / Protein: 9.3 g / Calories 110Kcal

BURRATA & ROASTED CAULIFLOWER

Burrata Cheese is keto-friendly fresh mozzarella cheese with the center of the ball filled with cream... drool!

Ingredients

- 2 tablespoons fresh thyme
- 1 (washed, trimmed, cored & sliced) large cauliflower head

- 1 teaspoon Celtic sea salt and fresh ground pepper
- 1 roasted garlic head
- 2 tablespoons coconut oil, melted

Garnish With

- 8 ounces burrata cheese (Alternatively you can use vegan burrata for a 100% plant-dish)

- 2 tablespoons fresh thyme

Instructions

1. Heat the oven to use to about 425°F.
2. Lay the cauliflower on a leveled layer in a rimmed baking sheet.
3. Sprinkle some melted coconut oil over the

cauliflower layer and add some salt, pepper and thyme leaves.

4. Press over the baking sheet mixture some soft roasted garlic.

5. Then toss the baking sheet content until it is properly combined.

6. Place into the preheated oven and bake till the cauliflower caramels slightly. Turn over the cauliflower just once while roasting.

7. Serve the roasted cauliflower and top it up with burrata cheese and fresh thyme.

Nutrition Facts

Serves: 8 Servings / Calories 150Kcal / Fat 11g / Protein 9g / Carbs 5g

VEGAN KOHLRABI

Kohlrabi vegetable might be new to you, but slitting it into pieces and making fries out of it gives good feeling!

Ingredients

- 1 tbsp vegan butter
- 2 crushed garlic cloves
- 2 kohlrabi (bottom removed, stalks trimmed, peeled & sliced into 1/4 thick pieces)
- Salt, as necessary
- Pepper, as necessary

Garnish With

- Parsley

Instructions

1. Fill the pot with water and boil over medium heat.
2. Add the kohlrabi pieces and cook for approximately 4-5 minutes until soft yet firm.
3. Drain the kohlrabi by making use of the colander, drench it under running cold water, and toss dry by using a paper towel.
4. Over medium heat, add vegan butter to a skillet.
5. Incorporate garlic in the skillet with melted butter

and cook until the aroma surrounds your kitchen.
6.   Add the salt and the slices of kohlrabi and pepper into the skillet.
7.   Turn the kohlrabi on all sides until golden brown.
8.   Serve and top with sliced parsley.

Nutrition Facts

Serves: 2 servings / Carbs 2.6g / Calories 100Kcal / Protein 6.2 grams / Fats 3.6 grams

BAKED PARMESAN ZUCCHINI ROUNDS

A simple recipe and winter side dish with cooked Parmesan zucchini rounds are rapidly combined with only two components and will vanish even more quickly from the table!

Ingredients

- 2 zucchini, medium-sized (washed, pat dried & sliced into 1/4" thick rounds)
- 1/2 cup vegan Parmesan cheese, freshly grated
- Garlic salt & freshly ground black pepper (if desired)

Instructions

1. Heat up the oven to about 425°F; divide the oven by placing an oven rack in the center of the oven.
2. Prepare and line the baking sheet to use with a parchment paper or foil (sparingly oiled with a cooking spray).
3. Arrange the zucchini rounds on the prepared and lined baking sheet.
4. Sprinkle lightly over the zucchini rounds some garlic salt and fresh ground black pepper.
5. Roll out some vegan parmesan across each zucchini round and move to the preheated oven.
6. Allow it to bake for about 15-20 minutes or until the vegan parmesan turns golden brown.

7. Serve and enjoy.

Nutrition Facts

Serves: 2-4 servings / Calories: 141kcal /
Carbohydrates: 7g / Protein: 11g / Fat: 7g

VEGAN BUTTER PECAN SANDWICH

These butter pecan protein bars is keto-friendly and contains less than a gram of sugar. The recipe has the taste of a creamy dessert. It's also gluten-free, vegan, milk-free, and rich in protein and fiber.

Ingredients

- 4 toasted pecan halves
- 1/2 tbsp unsalted vegan butter
- 1 pinch sea salt

Instructions

1. Lay out half of the vegan over 2 halves of pecan.
2. Sprinkle on each buttered pecan half a small amount of salt.
3. Place the pecan halves on top of each other.
4. Serve and enjoy.

Nutrition Facts

Serves: 2 servings / Calories 245kcal / Fat: 13.8g / Carbs: 14g / Protein: 20g

CHEESY BREAD TWISTS

Full with pesto and mozzarella, those twists are the perfect snack, but also a delicious side dish in healthy lunch or dinner.

Ingredients

- 1/4 cup coconut flour
- 1/2 cup almond flour
- 1 beaten egg
- 1/2 tsp salt
- 1 tsp baking powder
- 2 oz. butter
- 1/4 cup green pesto
- 6 + 1/2 oz. shredded mozzarella
- 1 beaten egg (for the top)

Instructions

1. Preheat the oven to 350°F.
2. In a large bowl, mix all the dry ingredients together, then combine the egg.
3. Melt the cheese and the butter in a pot on low heat. Mix until the batter is smooth.
4. Slowly add the cheese mix to the dry bowl and blend them together into a firm dough.
5. On a parchment paper, place the dough and use a rolling pin to make a rectangle, around 1/5" thick.
6. Spread pesto on top of it and cut into 1" strips. Twist and lay them on a baking sheet cover with parchment paper. Brush with the whisked egg.

7. Bake for around 15-20 minutes (Until they're golden brown). Serve and enjoy!

Nutrition Facts

Serves: 10 servings / Calories: 194 kcal / Carbohydrates: 1g / Protein: 8g/ Fat: 17g

PORTOBELLO MUSHROOMS STUFFED WITH CHEESE

The portobello mushrooms recipe is stuffed with meat and flavored cheese and roasted in olive oil. It's stocked with more cheese and heated until the cheese is bubbly and fully melted.

Ingredients

- Fresh thyme
- 2 cups lettuce
- 4 Portobello mushrooms (washed; remove & chop stems)
- 1 cup crumbled vegan blue cheese
- Salt, as necessary
- 2 tablespoons olive oil

Instructions

1. Heat the oven to use to about 350°F.
2. Sprinkle some salt on the mushrooms until satisfied.
3. Combine the sliced mushroom and the thyme new leaves in a mixing bowl.
4. Fill every mushroom caps with crumbled vegan blue cheese, chopped stems, and thyme.
5. Transfer and bake the mushroom in the preheated oven.
6. Let it bake for about 20-25 minutes before serving.
7. Toss some fresh green onions and olive oil together.

8. Top up the mushroom cheese with the green onion mixture and enjoy!

Nutrition Facts

Serves: 2 servings / Calories 195Kcal / Fat 16g / Carbohydrates 5g / Sugar 2g / Protein 9g

VEGAN CRACKERS

Crackers produced from almond flour are easy keto appetizers and perfect for low-carb dieters. These meal of almond flour crackers will resolve your craving for bread quickly if you miss bread as a keto or low carb dieter.

Ingredients

- 4 tablespoons hemp hearts
- 1/2 cup almond flour
- 4 tablespoons of chia seeds (soaked in 1/2 cup water for an hour)

- 2 tablespoons olive oil
- 1 pinch sea salt

Instructions

1. Heat the oven to use to about 200°F.
2. Soak and stir the jelly chia seeds until you reach the required consistency. The mixture should come out thick, if the seeds are watery or contain too much fluid, add one more tablespoon of chia seeds and put aside for about ten minutes.
3. Transfer the other ingredients into a large mixing bowl and mix until a dough-like consistency is achieved.
4. Shape the dough into a ball form and stack it on a big parchment paper piece.

5. Use a cling wrap plastic to cover the dough balls.
6. Use a bottle or a rolling pin to roll the covered dough balls until it achieves a soft texture.
7. Without breaking, the dough roll must be thinner than a quarter of an inch.
8. Remove your plastic wrap carefully if the dough is as consistent as it is desired.
9. Transfer to a large cookie sheet the rolled dough and move to the preheated furnace.
10. Allow it to bake for about 45 minutes or until the dough is mildly browned and drained. When you roll more than 1/4 inch thick the paste might not dry quickly; so if after the first 45 minutes you have trouble drying the dough, it's recommended that you remove the parchment paper and flip the mixture on the other side to dry.
11. Remove the dough from the heat as soon as it is crispy and dry.
12. Use a knife to slice the cooled dough into 2-inch pieces.
13. Remove the parchment paper from under the dough.
14. Store in a covered container and refrigerate.

Nutrition Facts

Serves: 8 Servings / Calories 50Kcal / Fat 4.3g / Carbohydrates 1.9g / Protein 1.9g

NOURISHING GINGER BAKED PLUMS

This recipe is a combination of orange, cinnamon, shrimp and ginger, at their best simplicity. Ideal for pudding or lunch.

Ingredients

- 5 (pitted) firm plums, washed & segmented into 8 pieces
- 1/2 teaspoon cinnamon
- 1 large orange, zested
- 2 peeled ginger, grated
- 5 tablespoons water
- 10-15 drops liquid stevia, as necessary

Serve With (If desired)

- 2-4 generous tbsps coconut yogurt per portion

Instructions

1. Heat the oven to use to about 375ºF.
2. Position the segmented plum over the baking tray.
3. Fill the mixing bowl with 1 tbsp water, cinnamon, orange zest, and grated ginger.
4. Stir to combine the cinnamon mixture with top plum.
5. Place the flesh of the plums facing side-down on the tray and move to the preheated oven.

6. Allow it to bake for 20 minutes or thereabout.
7. Serve straight away from the oven or let it cool.
8. Add coconut yogurt as a topping.

Nutrition Facts

Serves: 6 servings / Calories 29 kcal / Carbs 6.2 grams / Protein 0.5 grams / Fat 0.2 grams

RICED CAULIFLOWER STIR-FRY & CRISPY PEANUT TOFU

If you were looking for a suitable crucible, baked tofu recipe, this is definitely for you!

Ingredients

- 2 minced garlic cloves
- 12 oz. organic extra-firm tofu
- 1 tablespoon sesame oil, toasted
- Cauliflower Tofu
- 1 small cauliflower head

Sauce Ingredients

- 1/4 cup stevia
- 1/4 cup reduced-sodium soy sauce
- 1/2 teaspoon chili garlic sauce
- 1 + 1/2 tablespoons sesame oil, toasted
- 2 + 1/2 tablespoons almond butter (Alternatively peanut butter)

Add-Ins

- Top With sriracha, cilantro, fresh lime juice
- Mixed Veggies (broccoli, red pepper, green onion, baby bok choy)

Instructions

1. Wrap the tofu individually with a clean paper towel or an absorbent cloth and then place n heavy board or skillet over it for 15 minutes to drain out its moisture.
2. Heat up the oven to use to about 400°F.
3. Cut and shape the tofu into cubes and arrange in one single layer on a parchment paper-lined baking sheet.
4. In the preheated oven, place the baking sheets with lined cubes of tofu and allow it to bake for about 25 minutes until firm and dry.
5. Remove the baking sheet from the oven and set it aside to cool off.
6. Put all the sauce ingredients in a large mixing bowl and whip until adequately combined.
7. Season it and adjust the taste as needed.
8. Combine the tofu and sauce and mix until the tofu is fully coated.
9. Marinate for 15 minutes or more until flavors are blended.
10. Put cauliflower in a big grater or food processor.
11. Blend to reach rice-like consistency and let it settle down.
12. Prepare the veggies as required.
13. Over medium-high heat, add a blend of sesame oil and soy sauce in a large skillet.
14. Cook the veggies in the melted oil.
15. In a bowl, put the cooked veggies, and then cover it to keep them warm.

16. Add the tofu into the preheated skillet and mix with sauce mixture until fully coated.
17. Cook and continuously stir the tofu until it turns brown.
18. Take off the heat, move into a bowl, cover it with a lid, and let it sit for a while.
19. Scrape any residue off the skillet and rinse the pot under running hot water.
20. Place the tofu back in the oven.
21. Drizzle a few drops of sésame oil into the pan then incorporate the riced garlic and cauliflower.
22. Continue to stir till the mixture is combined correctly. Also, place a cover over the pan to steam the riced cauliflower.
23. Cook, occasionally stirring, until soft and browned, for five to eight minutes.
24. Add in the pot a few spoonfuls of the sauce to add taste.
25. Top with vegetables and tofu then serve.
26. Enjoy right away or keep it refrigerated for later use.

Nutrition Facts

Serves: 2 servings / Calories: 524Kcal / Fat: 34g / Carbohydrates: 38.5g / Protein: 24.5g

VEGAN SPICY CHOW CHOW

This spicy mixture of tomatoes, cabbage and peppers are traditionally eaten with beans, fresh vegetables or grilled meats.

Ingredients

- 1/2 cup white vinegar
- 1/4 teaspoon turmeric, ground
- 1 teaspoon yellow mustard seed
- 1 cup green cabbage, minced
- 1 (minced) small red bell pepper
- 1 (minced) Habanero pepper
- 1 (minced) little green bell pepper
- 1/2 tablespoon salt
- 1/2 cup + 2 tablespoons Swerve or Erythritol (granulated)
- 1/4 cup water
- 1 (minced) medium yellow onion

Instructions

1. Find a large jar and add water, swerve and other spices then mix everything together.
2. Over medium heat, add the vegetables into the pan.
3. Allow it to simmer for 20-30 minutes or until the veggies break down, and the blend gives a syrup-like consistency.

4. Set it aside and let it cool.
5. Move to a covered pot and refrigerate for later use.

Nutrition Facts

Serves: 8 servings / Carbs 2.9 grams /
Protein 0.6 grams / Fat 0.2 grams / Calories 21 kcal

VEGAN TAHINI SAUCED FALAFEL

This cauliflower falafel recipe is a low-carb and tasteful meal that gave me chills when I tried the first time.

Ingredients

- 1 teaspoon kosher salt
- 1 tablespoon cumin, ground
- 1/2 teaspoon cayenne pepper
- 1 cup pureed raw cauliflower (gotten from 1 medium head of cauliflower florets, blended in a food processor)
- 2 large eggs
- 1/2 tablespoon coriander, ground
- 1/2 cup slivered almonds, ground in a blender or food processor
- 3 tablespoons coconut flour
- 2 tablespoons chopped fresh parsley
- 1 minced garlic clove

Tahini Sauce Ingredients

- 1 tablespoon lemon juice
- 4 tablespoons water
- 1 teaspoon salt
- 2 tablespoons tahini paste
- 1 minced garlic clove

Instructions

1. In a fairly large jar, combine the ground cauliflower and ground almonds.

2. Mix well before incorporating the other ingredients, excluding the parts of the tahini sauce.
3. Continue to stir until the mixture is fully combined.
4. Over medium heat, add a half mixture of grapeseed oil and olive oil and any other light vegan oil into a saucepan.
5. Use your hand to form patties from the ground almond batter.
6. Work two sets in hot brown oil.
7. Cook the first part on one side for about 4 minutes or until the surfaces start turning brown and flip to boil the other hand.
8. Drain brown patties on a lined tray of parchment paper towel to let out any excess oil.
9. Combine all the tahini sauce components in a small bowl and mix them together. To dilute the sauce, add more water.
10. Serve the patties and top it with tomato, parsley and tahini sauce.

Nutrition Facts

Serving Size: 2 patties / Calories: 281Kcal / Fat: 24g / Carbohydrates: 5g / Protein: 8g

PORTOBELLO MUSHROOM TACOS

These vegetarian portobello grilled mushroom tacos provide the perfect summer lunch and are healthy, delicious and delightful.

Ingredients

- 1 tsp onion powder
- 1/4 cup mild or spicy harissa
- 3 tbsps (shared) olive oil
- 1 tsp cumin, ground
- 1 lb. portobello mushrooms (450g) {stems removed}
- 6 collard green leaves (rinsed & sturdy stems chopped off)

Guacamole Ingredients

- 1 tbsp cilantro, chopped
- Pinch of salt
- 1 + 1/2-2 tbsps lime or lemon juice
- 2 medium ripe avocados (halved, pitted & flesh scooped out)
- 2 tbsp red onion, chopped
- 2 tbsps tomatoes, chopped

Top With (If desired)

- Cashew cream
- Cilantro, chopped
- Tomatoes, chopped

Instructions

1. Clean the mushrooms and pat dry them.
2. Find a small mixing bowl and add 1 + 1/2 tablespoons of olive oil, onion powder, cumin, and harissa.
3. Stir the mixture until adequately combined.
4. Transfer the mushrooms into the onion harissa mix and toss until the fungus is fully coated. All the sides of the mushroom should be totally covered.
5. Allow the covered mushrooms to marinate by setting it aside for 15 minutes.
6. While the mushroom is getting marinated, mash the avocado in a pot and add salt, lime or lemon juice, red onion, sliced tomatoes, and cilantro.
7. Stir continually until fully mixed.
8. Over medium-high heat, add the reserved 1/2 tbsps of olive oil into a skillet or saute pan.
9. Put marinated mushrooms into the saute pan for 3 minutes before flipping.
10. Flip it to the other side and saute for a further 2-3 minutes until evenly browned.
11. Turn off the heat and let mushrooms cool down for 2-3 minutes then cut into slices.
12. Fill every collard green leaf with few slices of the cooked mushrooms.
13. Top each collard green leaves with chopped tomatoes, cashew, cilantro, and guacamole.
14. Serve and enjoy.

Nutrition Facts

Serves: 3 servings / Calories 307Kcal / Fat 11.3g /
Carbohydrate 41.5g / Protein 9.4g

PECAN CINNAMON PORRIDGE

It is a good lunch, which even without sweeteners tastes excellent. It's satisfying and will keep hunger cravings away!

Ingredients

- 1/2 teaspoon cinnamon
- 1/4 cup toasted coconut, unsweetened
- 1-2 tablespoons Swerve, or Erythritol or 5-10 drops liquid stevia if desired
- 3/4 cup unsweetened almond milk
- 1/4 cup walnuts or pecans, chopped
- 1/4 cup (preferably roasted) almond butter
- 1/4 cup coconut milk
- 1 tablespoon coconut oil
- 2 tablespoons hemp seeds
- 2 tablespoons whole chia seeds

Instructions

1. Over med-heat, combine almond milk, coconut milk, coconut oil and almond butter in a small saucepan.
2. Stir, and allow the dough to simmer until it grows hot.
3. Turn off the heat and add chopped pecans, hemp seeds, stevia, cinnamon, chia seeds and toasted coconut (reserve some for later use).

4. Stir continuously until the dough is fully combined, then set it aside for 5-10 minutes.
5. Incorporate the pecan cinnamon porridge into serving dishes and top it up with the reserved toasted coconut.
6. Serve hot or cold.

Nutrition Facts

Serves: 2 servings / Carbs 5.2 grams / Protein 13.8 grams / Fat 51.7 grams / Calories 582 kcal

DELICIOUS GUACAMOLE

It is the most exceptional guacamole recipe you'll find anywhere since it's easy to prepare. Authentic guacamole contains no unnecessary fillers and ingredients.

Ingredients

- 1/2 teaspoon cinnamon
- 1/4 cup toasted coconut, unsweetened
- 1-2 tablespoons Swerve, or Erythritol or 5-10 drops liquid stevia if desired
- 3/4 cup unsweetened almond milk
- 1/4 cup walnuts or pecans, chopped
- 1/4 cup (preferably roasted) almond butter
- 1/4 cup coconut milk
- 1 tablespoon coconut oil
- 2 tablespoons hemp seeds
- 2 tablespoons whole chia seeds

Instructions

1. Put the first of the skinned avocados in a bowl, mash with a fork and set aside the other avocado.
2. Add the diced tomatoes, crushed garlic, finely sliced chili peppers, lime juice, finely chopped onion and to the bowl.
3. Use a fork to mix the content of the bowl together.

4. Cut the extra avocado into 1/2 inch pieces and set aside. Add to the content of the bowl some fresh cilantro, reserves of the diced avocado, pepper and salt. Stir continuously until it is fully mixed. Serve with desired toppings and garnishes.

Nutrition Facts

Servings: 4 Servings / Calories: 184.8kcal / Carbohydrates: 12.3g / Protein: 2.5g / Fat: 15.8g

SESAME CARROT FALAFEL

Falafel is traditionally made with chickpeas and is a no go area if you're on paleo or low-carb diet.

Ingredients

- 1/2 teaspoon cinnamon
- 1/4 cup toasted coconut, unsweetened
- 1-2 tablespoons Swerve, or Erythritol or 5-10 drops liquid stevia if desired
- 3/4 cup unsweetened almond milk
- 1/4 cup walnuts or pecans, chopped
- 1/4 cup (preferably roasted) almond butter
- 1/4 cup coconut milk
- 1 tablespoon coconut oil
- 2 tablespoons hemp seeds
- 2 tablespoons whole chia seeds

Instructions

1. Heat up the oven to use to about 400°F.
2. In a baking tray, add 1 tsp of olive oil and garlic.
3. Put it in the preheated oven and allow it to bake for 12 minutes or until soft.
4. Remove from the oven and peel it.
5. In a bowl of boiling water, add the sliced carrots into the hot water.
6. Steam the sliced carrots for about 18 minutes or until soft.

7. Take the carrots from the water and set it aside to cool.
8. Use an electric blender or any other available food processor to blend the pickled pepper, salt, 1/2 fine chopped coriander, tahini, coconut flour, citrus juice, 3 tbsps of olive oil, ground coriander, cumin, peeled garlic, and carrots.
9. Continue to blend until the ingredients are fully combined. Scrub off the loosen stuck bits from inside of the food processor and blend for more minutes until a near consistency is achieved.
10. Tuck the other half of the chopped coriander.
11. Shape the product of the mixture into falafel-like balls with your clean hands.
12. Pour sesame seeds over the falafel-like balls and then transfer into the baking tray lined with parchment paper.
13. Lightly coat the falafel balls with olive oil and move it into the preheated oven.
14. Bake one side for about 10 minutes, flip to the other, and bake for another 10 minutes. The end product should be golden colored.
15. Serve and enjoy.

Nutrition Facts

Serves: 4 servings / Carbs 11.6 grams /
Protein 5.4 grams / Fat 22.5 grams / Calories 292 kcal

LOW-CARB ONION RINGS

Everyone loves onion rings. They are delicius and addicting, so why don't you enjoy this keto version? Easy, tasty, and low on carb!

Ingredients

- 1 large onion
- 1 egg
- 1 cup almond flour
- 1 + 1/2 oz. grated parmesan cheese
- 1 tsp garlic powder
- 1 tbsp chili powder (Alternatively paprika powder)
- 1 pinch salt
- 1 tbsp olive oil

Instructions

1. Preheat the oven to 400°F.
2. Peel the onion and then slice it into rings, around 1/5".
3. Get two bowls. In one mix all dry ingredients, in the other one whisk the egg.
4. Dip the onion rings (one at the time) in the egg mixture, then in the flour batter.
5. Cover a baking sheet with parchment paper, then lay the rings on it.
6. Spread the oil on the rings, then bake in the oven for about 15-20 minutes (When crisp and gold brown, they're ready)

Nutrition Facts

Serves: 1 servings / Calories: 289kcal /
Carbohydrates: 5g / Protein: 12g/ Fat: 23g

VEGETARIAN KETO DINNER RECIPES

At dinner, we can relax after a long day of work and enjoy a tasty and relax full meal...usually. Whatever is the case, here are some recipes that can fit a dinner with friends, on your own and any other possible occasion, obviously 100% keto-veggie!

KETO PASTA WITH BLUE CHEESE SAUCE

It's easy to feel the lack of creamy, exquisite taste of pasta when you follow a keto diet. With this version of one Italy's most favorite, you won't give up the flavor, even on a low carb and healthy diet.

Ingredients

Blue cheese sauce

- 2 oz. butter
- 7 oz. cream cheese
- 2 pinches pepper
- 7 oz. blue cheese

Pasta

- 1 tsp salt
- 8 eggs
- 10 oz. cream cheese
- 5 + 1/2 tbsp ground psyllium husk powder

For serving

- 4 tbsp roasted pine nuts
- 1 + 1/2 oz. grated parmesan cheese

Instructions

Pasta

1. Preheat the oven to 300°F.
2. Whisk eggs, then mix cream cheese and salt until

obtaining a smooth batter. Continue to blend while stirring in the psyllium husk, a little at a time. Let rest for about 2 minutes.

3. With a spatula, spread the batter on a baking sheet, previously covered with parchment paper. Put another piece of parchment paper on top of the mixture and flatten it with a rolling pin until it is around 13 x 18 inches.

4. Place the batter (covered with parchment paper) in the oven, and bake for around 10-12 minutes. Remove the paper after it has cooled down.

5. Using a knife or with kitchen scissors, cut the pasta into thin strips.

6. The pasta can be stored for 2-3 days in the refridgerator (you can also freeze it).

7. Use the pasta at room temperature, and let the warm sauce heat it (the pasta is already cooked).

Blue cheese sauce

1. Using a small saucepan, over medium heat, gently melt the blue cheese, while stirring regularly. Add cream cheese, and keep on stirring for a few minutes.

2. Add the butter, and stir until smooth. Do not boil; it has just to be hot.

3. While still hot, serve with your keto pasta. Add a unique flavor by topping with grated parmesan and roasted pine nuts.

Nutrition Facts

Serves: 1 servings / Calories: 943kcal /
Carbohydrates: 10g / Protein: 35g/ Fat: 84g

COCONUT WHIPPED CREAM BERRY BOWL

This is a recipe for a healthy and vegan Berry Bowl with Whipped Coconut Cream.

Ingredients

- 4 cups your desired fresh berries
- 5 (minced) fresh mint leaves + additional for garnish
- 1 whole vanilla pod
- 1 tsp birch xylitol
- 1 can (chilled) full-fat coconut milk

Instructions

1. Slice the mixed berries into small chunks and pour them into a large mixing bowl.
2. Add minced mint leaves to berries and toss until well combined then set aside.
3. Scoop chilled coconut milk into a large bowl.
4. Slice the ends of the vanilla pod laterally with a paring knife.
5. Remove seeds from the vanilla pod using the knife's edge and pour it into the bowl of coconut cream.
6. Whisk the mixture slowly until combined using a hand mixer.
7. Add birch xylitol into the mixture after whisking for 1 minute.

159

8. Mix until it feels like fluffy whipped cream.
9. Use the whipped cream as toppings for the berries.
10. Garnish with extra mint and serve.

Nutrition Facts

Serves: 4-6 servings / Carbs 8.5 grams /
Protein 2.1 grams / Fat 12 grams / Calories 156 kcal

RASPBERRY CHIA PUDDING

This is a vegan and gluten-free recipe. Chia Puddings are great because you can whip them up in little time.

Ingredients

- 1 cup frozen or fresh raspberries
- Stevia, Swerve or Erythritol, as necessary
- 1/2 cup whole chia seeds
- 1 cup coconut milk
- 1/2 cup water
- 2-3 teaspoons unsweetened vanilla extract or 1 teaspoon vanilla powder

Instructions

1. Add water, raspberries and coconut milk into a food processor.
2. Leave some raspberries for use as a topping.
3. Blend until a smooth consistency is achieved.
4. Add desired sweetener, raspberry milk, vanilla, and the chia seeds in mixing bowl and leave for 25-30 minutes in a refrigerator.
5. Serve into glasses and use the remaining raspberries as toppings.
6. Is it possible to conserve it in the fridge for up to 3 days.

Nutrition Facts

Serves: 4 servings / Calories: 342kcal /
Carbohydrates: 49g / Protein: 9g / Fat: 15g

TOFU NUGGETS

This is a vegan version of Chick-fil-A nuggets. The tofu nuggets are baked and crispy and are perfect for everyone.

Ingredients

- Vegan sriracha mayo (sriracha + 1/4 cup vegan mayo)
- 1 tsp (equal amounts of rosemary mix, sage, thyme, ginger, oregano, and marjoram)
- 1/4 cup vegetable oil
- 1/2 tsp cayenne pepper
- 2 cups vegan broth
- 1 tsp salt
- 1/2 tsp minced onion, dried
- 1/2 tsp garlic, dried
- 3 tbsps nutritional yeast
- 1/2 cup all-purpose flour
- 1 (14 oz.) extra-firm tofu package, drained, frozen & then thawed
- 1/2 tsp black pepper, freshly ground

Instructions

1. Slice thawed tofu into cubes.
2. Transfer the cubes into a shallow pan and pour vegan broth until tofu is fully immersed.
3. Let it marinate for around 8 hours, or leave overnight in the refrigerator.
4. Add some sriracha into 1/4 cup of vegan mayo.
5. Keep stirring until totally mixed.

6. Add more sriracha as desired.
7. Add pepper, spices, salt, flour, yeast, and marinated tofu into a bowl and toss until tofu is completely covered.
8. Heat the oil in a big skillet over medium to low heat.
9. Transfer the coated tofu into the hot and melted oil.
10. Cook every side for 2-3 minutes until browned and crisp.
11. Remove the skillet and place on a wire rack to drain.
12. Serve with vegan sriracha mayo mixture.

Nutrition Facts

Serves: 3 Servings / Calories 134Kcal / Fat 8.8g / Carbohydrate 22.4g / Protein 11.7g

BAKED STRAWBERRY POTS

Have you previously attempted to bake strawberries? They are lovely. A great idea of whether or not your fruits have gone by, and need to be used.

Ingredients

- 1.2 ounces 35g almonds, flaked
- Pinch salt
- Almond Crumb
- 14.1 ounces (400g) coconut yogurt
- 10.6 ounces (300g) strawberries (stalks removed & halved or quartered)
- 1 tablespoon water
- 3/4 tsp vanilla powder or 1 vanilla pod (split open)
- 1/2 lemon, juiced
- 3.2 ounces (90g) almonds, ground
- 1/3 cup coconut flakes, unsweetened
- 1 teaspoon vanilla powder

Instructions

1. Add vanilla, water, and lemon juice into the strawberry pieces.
2. Place into oven and roast until tender, for about 15 minutes.
3. Remove the strawberry mix from oven and leave to cool.
4. Add vanilla, salt, flaked and ground almonds on a separate baking tray.

5. Mix till combined and transfer into the oven. Let it toast until golden, for about 15 minutes.
6. Add coconut chips into the almond mixture at the 12 minutes mark and roast till initial 15 minute cook time is up. This way, the coconut chips will cook for up to 3 minutes.
7. Add the strawberry mixture into a small bowl then top with coconut yogurt.
8. Sprinkle almond crumb on top of the strawberry yogurt mix.
9. Serve and eat.

Nutrition Facts

Serves: 5 servings / Carbs 9.1 grams /
Protein 13.6 grams / Fat 20 grams / Calories 277 kcal

SPAGHETTI SQUASH

This delicious dish is a funny and innovative way of cooking spaghetti. Try it out, and you won't be disappointed!

Ingredients

- 1 large spaghetti squash (halved lengthwise or widthwise with a chef's knife and seeded)
- Salt, as needed
- 1-2 tablespoons olive oil or coconut oil

Instructions

1. Preheat your oven to 400°F.
2. Use coconut or olive oil to coat your seeded and halved spaghetti squash.
3. Add salt to the spaghetti squash as desired.
4. Use aluminum foil to cover the spaghetti to prevent burning at the top before thoroughly cooked.
5. Place the spaghetti squash into a preheated oven and leave for 30 minutes. The cook time is based on the quantity of squash.
6. Peel off foil and cook for 10-20 more minutes.
7. Move the cooked spaghetti squash to a cooling rack and leave to sit for 5-10 minutes.

8. Scoop the strings of spaghetti from squash using a fork and transfer into a bowl.
9. Add desired toppings and sauces.
10. You can refrigerate for up to 5 days and freeze in plastic bags for 180 days.

Nutrition Facts

Serves: 1-2 servings / Carbs 9.1 grams /
Protein 13.6 grams / Fat 20 grams / Calories 277 kcal

BAKED BADRIJANI

This Georgian dish is made with fried eggplant and stuffed with spiced walnut paste

Ingredients

- 1/2 teaspoon apple cider vinegar
- Salt and pepper, as necessary
- 2 garlic cloves
- 1/2 lemon, juiced
- 3/4 cup walnuts
- 1/3 cup water
- 2 tablespoons olive oil
- 2 (fresh & firm) large eggplants, stalks removed & sliced into 1/4 thick pieces lengthways
- 1/8 teaspoon fenugreek
- Eggplant
- Pinch of sea salt
- 1/4 cup olive oil
- 1 teaspoon coriander, ground
- Walnut-Garlic Filling

Serve With

- 1 tablespoon cilantro, freshly chopped
- 1/4 cup fresh pomegranate seeds

Instructions

1. Preheat oven to 375°F.
2. After you have coated the slices of eggplant with

olive oil, transfer to a baking tray lined with parchment paper.

3. Place the eggplants in the oven and leave for 10 minutes on each side, until softened.
4. Flip the sides and cook for another 10 minutes.
5. Add walnut-garlic filling into a high powered electric blender.
6. Blend until totally smooth and lumps less.
7. Take out cooked eggplants from oven and leave to cool.
8. Use 1 tsp of walnut paste to coat each eggplant slice.
9. Sprinkle a pinch of fresh cilantro and some pomegranate seeds.
10. Roll the eggplants and top with leftover pomegranate seeds and cilantro.
11. Serve and enjoy.

Nutrition Facts

Serves: 4 servings / Carbs 5.7 grams /
Protein 4 grams / Fat 32.8 grams / Calories 334 kcal

TIKKA MASALA

This low-carb recipe contains soft cauliflower in a rich, creamy sauce. It's a vibrant red color and has lots of spices.

Ingredients

- 1 teaspoon garam masala
- 1/2 teaspoon cayenne pepper
- 1 teaspoon cumin, ground
- 1 tablespoon olive oil
- 1/2 teaspoon salt
- 1 (cut into small florets) cauliflower head

Sauce Ingredients

- 1/2 diced white onion
- 1/2 teaspoon cayenne pepper
- 1/4 cup cilantro, minced
- 4 tablespoons coconut oil (Alternatively unsalted vegan butter)
- 2 minced garlic cloves
- 1/2 teaspoon salt
- 1/2 cup coconut cream
- 1 + 1/2 teaspoons paprika
- 1 tablespoon ginger, minced
- 1 tablespoon garam masala
- 1/2 cup water
- 1 + 1/2 cups tomatoes, crushed
- 1 teaspoon cumin, ground

171

Instructions

1. Preheat oven to 425°F.
2. Mix spices, oil and the cauliflower in a large bowl and toss them until well coated.
3. Arrange the cauliflower on a foil-lined baking sheer.
4. Transfer into a heated oven and leave for 30 minutes or until softened.
5. Pour either coconut oil or vegan butter into a deep skillet on medium to high heat.
6. Add garlic, ginger, and onion to the hot oil and leave for about 5 minutes, until the onion starts to turn caramel.
7. Add the spices into the veggie mixture and let it cook for 30 seconds.
8. Pour cream, water, and tomatoes into the hot oil and allow it to simmer for 10 minutes while stirring from time to time.
9. Add the cooked cauliflower into the oil skillet with cream.
10. Mix until thoroughly combined and serve.

Nutrition Facts

Serves: 5 servings / Calories 302Kcal / Fat: 21 grams / Carbs: 4.8 grams / Protein: 24.8 grams

CHOCOLATE ORANGE CHIA PUDDING

This dish is perfect for dinner and dessert and takes little time to prepare.

Ingredients

- 1/2 teaspoon fresh orange zest or a few orange oil drops
- 1/4 cup coconut milk
- 2 tablespoons 85% dark chocolate
- 1/4 cup (ground or whole) chia seeds
- 5-10 drops orange stevia extract
- 1/2 cup almond milk or water
- 1 tablespoon powdered Swerve or Erythritol

Top With (If Desired)

- Coconut cream

Instructions

1. Mix stevia, erythritol, fresh orange zest, coconut milk, almond milk or water, and chia seeds into a mixing bowl and stir.
2. Leave the dough to sit for at least 15 minutes.
3. Mix chopped dark chocolate chips or grated dark chocolate until combined.
4. Or top with grated dark chocolate, vegan whipped cream and orange zest.

5. It's ready to eat.

Nutrition Facts

Serves: 2 servings / Calories: 175Kcal / Fat: 2g /
Carbohydrates: 21g / Protein: 5g

BABA GANOUSH

This recipe is a roasted eggplant dip or baba ganoush. It's flavored with garlic, tahini, cumin, and olive oil. It can be served alongside grilled cheese, tofu, and vegetables.

Ingredients

- 1 lemon, juiced
- 1/4 cup light tahini
- 1/2 teaspoon chili flakes (Alternatively 1/4 teaspoon chili powder)
- 2 tablespoons fresh parsley (plus additional for garnish)
- 1/2 teaspoon salt
- 3 tablespoons olive oil
- 1/2 teaspoon cumin, ground
- 3 medium eggplants
- 2 crushed garlic cloves

Serve With

- Keto cheesy crackers
- Garnish With
- Keto breadsticks
- Paprika
- Freshly cut vegetables (cucumber, red pepper, celery stalks)

Instructions

1. Place the eggplants on strong parchment paper or baking sheet liner with foil.
2. Pierce the eggplants severally with a fork.
3. Put under a broiler until the skin starts to get slightly charred. This should take 6-8 minutes.

4. Turn the eggplants over at half the cook time.
5. Remove from grill and heat up the oven to 430°F.
6. Move the eggplants into the oven and leave until its inside is softened and wrinkly (about 30-40 minutes).
7. Scoop the fleshy part of the eggplant out and dispose of the stems and skins.
8. Sieve flesh with a colander or sieve to remove excess juice.
9. Mix all other ingredients but the paprika and olive oil with the eggplant flesh.
10. Share into serving bowls and sprinkle with ground paprika and fresh parsley, and drizzle olive oil on everything.
11. Enjoy it right away or refrigerate for up to 5 days.

Nutrition Facts

Serves: 8 servings / Calories: 81kcal / Carbohydrates: 6.3g / Protein: 2.3g / Fat: 6g

VEGAN RICH GRANOLA

This is a delicious low carb cereal that can also be served as a crunchy keto breakfast. They're vegan, sugar-free, grain-free and gluten-free.

Ingredients

- 1/2 cup flax meal
- 2 teaspoons orange zest (can be dried)
- 1/2 cup sunflower seeds
- 1/4 teaspoon cardamom
- 1 + 1/4 cup whole almonds (with the skin on)
- 1/2 teaspoon cinnamon
- 1/4 cup stevia, Swerve or erythritol
- 1/4 cup slivered almonds
- 1 cup unsweetened coconut, shaved or shredded
- 1/2 cup coconut oil
- 1/4 cup sesame seeds
- 1/2 cup pecans
- 1/2 cup pepitas
- 1/4 cup pinenuts
- 1/4 cup cashews
- 1/2 teaspoon vanilla powder

Instructions

1. Preheat oven to 300°F.
2. Roll a baking tray with parchment paper.
3. Add all spices, nuts, and seeds but the orange zest and salt into a large mixing bowl.

177

4. Stir until well blended.
5. Heat and melt coconut oil in a small pan.
6. Add stevia into hot coconut oil and mix.
7. Pour melted oil mixture into the nuts and seed mixture and stir until completely blended.
8. Spread nuts and seeds mix on the prepared baking tray.
9. Put the baking tray into a preheated oven and leave for 60 minutes.
10. Keep stirring every 15 minutes and make sure it doesn't burn, especially when it's been in the oven for 45 minutes.
11. Take out from the oven once it's crunchy and brown.
12. Leave granola to cool.
13. Sprinkle the orange zest and sea salt all over granola while it's still warm and stirs.
14. Once the granola is cool, store in a well-covered container and put in a cool, dry place for as long as 30 days.
15. Serve with cashew milk, coconut milk, and unsweetened almond milk.

Nutrition Facts

Serves: 12-24 Servings / Calories 166Kcal / Fat 14.6g / Carbohydrates 7g / Protein 4.8g

VEGAN STRAWBERRY CHIA JARS

These are tasty low-carb breakfasts that don't need any form of sweeteners. The strawberries and cinnamon present give a natural sweetness. The full-fat yogurt will add a refreshing taste.

Ingredients

Chia Layer

- 1 cup coconut milk
- 4 tablespoons whole chia seeds
- Liquid Stevia, as necessary (if desired)
- 1/4 teaspoon cinnamon
- 1/4 teaspoon ground ginger

Yogurt & Strawberry Layer

- 4 (sliced) large strawberries
- 1 cup coconut yogurt or creamed coconut milk

Strawberry Layer

- Liquid Stevia, as necessary, if desired
- 1 cup strawberries, sliced
- 2 tablespoons water

179

Instructions

Strawberry Layer

1. Pour 2 tbsps of water and 1 cup of diced strawberries into a saucepan over medium heat.
2. Let it simmer and cook for a few minutes or until soft.
3. Use spatula or fork to mash strawberries and let it sit.
4. Add a few drops of stevia, if desired

Chia Layer

1. Add a few drops of stevia,(optional), ginger powder, cinnamon, coconut milk and the chia seeds into a small mixing bowl.
2. Stir until well mixed.
3. Leave the mixture to soak for 30 minutes.
4. Scoop chia mixture into four jars.
5. Top the chia mixture with the cooked strawberry layer

Yogurt & Strawberry Layer

1. Add creamed coconut milk or yogurt on top of the chia pudding in the jars.
2. Use remaining slices of strawberry as toppings.
3. Refrigerate for up to 3 days.

Nutrition Facts

Serves: 4 servings / Carbs 7.5 grams /
Protein 8.7 grams / Fat 17.9 grams / Calories 230 kcal

KETO CEREAL

This is a simple homemade keto cereal that is gluten /sugar-free and healthy and needs only a few ingredients.

Ingredients

- 1/2 cup sunflower seed butter (blended sunflower seeds)
- 1-2 teaspoon vanilla powder or cocoa powder or cinnamon
- 20-30 drops liquid stevia
- 1/4 cup hemp hearts or pumpkin seeds or sesame seeds
- 1 cup unsweetened coconut, shredded
- 1/4 teaspoon salt
- Cereal
- 1/4 cup coconut milk
- 1/2 cup (ground or whole) chia seeds
- 1/4 cup water

Serve with

- Coconut milk
- Almond milk
- Frozen or fresh berries
- Coconut yogurt

Instructions

1. Add sunflower seed butter, cinnamon, salt or cocoa or vanilla powder, shredded coconuts and hemp hearts into a food processor.
2. Blend a little until the mixture is combined. Don't over blend the mixture.

3. Pour water, sweetener, coconut milk, and chia seeds into the processor.
4. Blend for a few more seconds and set aside for 15 minutes.
5. Preheat oven to 275°F.
6. Divide the solidified chia seeds mix between 2 baking sheets lined with parchment paper.
7. Spread the dough with a spatula until it's 1/3 thick. Cover the dough with another parchment paper and spread with a rolling pin until thin consistency is achieved.
8. Transfer both baking sheets into the oven and bake for 30 minutes until crisp.
9. Remove from the oven and use a sharp knife to cut into 1 square.
10. Leave for up to 15 minutes to crisp up and cool down.
11. Serve with berry toppings, yogurt or almond milk, coconut milk or cream.
12. The cereals can be stored for up to 14 days.

Nutrition Facts

Serves: 8 servings / Calories 190kcal / Fat 16.5g / Carbohydrates 7.3g / Protein 5.9g

KETO-VEGGIE BURGER

You've always thought that cannot exist a good burger without meat? Think again! This vegetarian, low-carb version, will let your mouth watering!

Ingredients

- 1/2 cup celery, finely chopped
- 1/2 cup onion, finely diced
- 1 tsp dried parsley
- 1 tbsp chia seeds
- 1 tbsp olive oil
- 2 minced cloves garlic
- 8 oz. mushrooms, stemmed and chopped
- 10 oz. bag frozen riced cauliflower
- 1 tsp Worcestershire sauce
- 1/2 tsp sea salt
- 1/4 tsp smoked paprika
- 1/4 tsp cumin
- 1/4 tsp garlic powder
- 1/4 cup flax meal
- 4 oz. grated sharp white cheddar cheese

Instructions

1. Warm olive oil in a large non-stick skillet, over medium heat, then add garlic, onions, and celery. Grill for around 2 minutes, or till onions start to soften. Add riced cauliflower and mushrooms. Stirring occasionally, cook for an additional 10-12 minutes, then remove the pan from heat.

2. Preheat the oven to 400°F.

3. While stirring, add Worcestershire sauce, cumin, salt, parsley, paprika, and garlic powder to the veggie mixture. Use then the shredded cheese, and mix until it has melted and is fully incorporated. Add the chia seeds and the flax meal, and stir until thoroughly combined. Put away from the heat and set aside to cool and thicken.

4. Get a baking sheet and line it with parchment paper. Once the blend is cold enough, divide it into 6 patties and lay them on the baking sheet.

5. Bake the veggie burgers for around 30 minutes (you want them to be nicely browned and with a crispy exterior. Chill for at least 5 minutes before serving. Enjoy!

Nutrition Facts

Serves: 6 servings / Calories: 161 kcal / Carbohydrates: 8g / Protein: 8g/ Fat: 11g

SWEET POTATO CASSEROLE WITH PECAN TOPPING

This is a Vegan Sweet Potato Casserole with a delicious pecan crust as a topping. It can be enjoyed as a thanksgiving classic.

Ingredients

- 1/4 tsp cloves
- 4 tbsps vegan butter softened
- 1 cup pumpkin, mashed
- 1 tsp nutmeg
- 1/2 tsp ginger
- 1 cauliflower head, steamed

- 3/4 tsp stevia drops
- 1/2 tsp salt
- 1 tsp cinnamon
- 3 flax eggs (3 tbsp flaxmeal + 9 tbsps hot water), combined separately and set aside for 10 minutes

Topping Ingredients

- 2 tbsps coconut flour
- 3 tbsps vegan brown sugar substitute
- 4 tbsps softened vegan butter

- 3 tbsps almond flour
- 3/4 cup pecans, chopped

Instructions

1. Preheat your oven to 325°F.
2. Add your cauliflower florets in a pressure cooker and steam for 5 minutes or until soft.

3. Add cloves, nutmeg, ginger, vegan butter, cinnamon, salt, sweetener, flax eggs, and pumpkin to the steamed cauliflower and blend together until a smooth consistency is achieved.
4. Transfer the blended mixture into an 11 X 17 or 2 qt. casserole dish.
5. Add the almond flour, brown sugar substitute, coconut flour, into a big bowl.
6. Then add the butter and pecans.
7. Stir until thoroughly mixed then sprinkle all over the cauliflower mix.
8. Transfer the casserole dish into the oven and bake for 30 minutes or until the topping is browned.
9. Serve and enjoy.

Nutrition Facts

Serves: 10 servings / Calories 271kcal / Fat 11g / Carbohydrates 39g / Protein 3g

ARTICHOKE SPINACH CASSEROLE

This is a popular dish that has become a yummy Keto-friendly casserole with mozzarella cheese on top.

Ingredients

- 1 tablespoon baking powder
- 6 oz. chopped artichoke hearts (drained)
- 5 oz. chopped fresh spinach
- 1/2 teaspoon pepper
- 3/4 cup coconut flour
- 8 flax eggs (8 tbsps flaxmeal + 24 tbsps hot water)
- 1 cup vegan parmesan, grated or nutritional yeast
- 3 minced garlic cloves
- 1 teaspoon salt
- 3/4 cup almond milk, unsweetened

Instructions

1. Pour 8 tbsps flaxmeal + 24 tbsps hot water into a small bowl and set aside.
2. Add salt, pepper, garlic, 1/2 cup of grated vegan parmesan or nutritional yeast, spinach, artichoke hearts, flax eggs, and almond milk into a big mixing bowl.
3. Whisk until well blended then add baking powder and coconut flour.

4. Mix until incorporated.
5. Set the flour mixture in a greased crock pot and scatter the reserved 1/2 cup of parmesan on top of the flour mixture.
6. Cook for 4-6 hours using low heat or 2-3 hours on high heat.
7. Use freshly chopped basil as toppings.
8. Serve and enjoy.

Nutrition Facts

Serves: 10 servings / Calories 493kcal / Fat 35g / Carbohydrates 7g / Protein 37g

HEMP HEART PORRIDGE

This keto grain-free porridge is made only with nuts and seeds. It's a full meal that's sugar-free, gluten-free, dairy-free, and vegan, paleo and keto.

Ingredients

- 1 cup vegan (coconut or almond) milk
- 1 tbsp chia seeds
- 2 tbsps flax seed, freshly ground
- 1/2 cup hemp hearts
- 1/2 tsp cinnamon, ground
- 3/4 tsp pure vanilla extract
- 1/4 cup almond flour or almonds, crushed
- 5 drops (no-alcohol) stevia

Top With

- 3 Brazil nuts
- 1 tbsp hemp hearts

Instructions

1. Add all the ingredients but the ground almonds and toppings in a small saucepan over med-heat.
2. Mix thoroughly.
3. Cook until slightly boiling.
4. Stir and leave until mixture is just bubbling, then cook for 1-2 minutes.
5. Switch off the heat and stir in crushed almonds.
6. Eat with 1 tbsp hemp hearts and Brazil nuts.

Nutrition Facts

Serves: 1 serving / Calories 374kcal / Fat 33g /
Carbohydrates 9g / Protein 11g

RASPBERRY LEMON DELICIOUS ROLLS

This delicious dough is lemon flavored and has lemon zest in it. It's also filled with raspberry jam.

Ingredients

Filling

- 1 teaspoon lemon extract
- 2 tablespoons (room temperature) vegan butter
- 1 teaspoon lemon juice
- 4 ounce (room temperature) vegan cream cheese
- 1/2 teaspoon vanilla extract
- 1 lemon, zested (approx. 2 tsps)
- 2 tablespoons stevia

Dough

- 1 flax egg (1 tbsp flaxmeal + 3 tbsps hot water), combined separately and set aside for 10 minutes
- 1/4 cup stevia
- 1 cup fine almond flour
- 1/4 tsp xanthan gum
- 1 + 1/4 tsps baking powder
- 2 cups part-skim vegan mozzarella cheese
- 1 tsp vanilla extract

Raspberry Sauce

- 1/2 cup frozen raspberries
- 1 tbsp water
- 2 tbsps stevia
- 1/4 tsp xanthan gum
- 2 tsps lemon juice

Lemon Glaze (if desired)

- 1/4 tsp vanilla extract
- 1 + 1/2 tbsps (room temperature) almond milk, unsweetened
- 2 tbsps stevia
- 2 tbsps (room temperature) vegan butter
- 1/2 oz. (room temperature) cream cheese
- 1/4 tsp lemon extract
- 1 tsp lemon juice

Instructions

Filling

1. Mix lemon juice, lemon extract, lemon zest, sweetener, vanilla extract, and the vegan cream cheese in a bowl and blend with electric mixer till it's smooth and even.

Raspberry Sauce

1. Add sweetener and xanthan gum into a medium saucepan and whisk until thoroughly mixed.
2. Slowly add lemon juice and water to the saucepan mixture and continue whisking.
3. Put a saucepan on medium to low heat and add

raspberries to the saucepan mixture and continue to stir.

4. Cook until it simmers and let it sit.

Dough

1. Preheat oven to 350°F.
2. Use vegan butter or coconut oil to grease a 9 inch round pan.
3. Pour about 2" of water into the lower part of double boiler on high heat.
4. Let the water simmer before reducing heat to low heat.
5. Mix in sweetener, baking powder, almond flour, and xanthan gum, in the top part of a double boiler.
6. Stir in the flax egg mixture and vanilla extract into the mixture until blended. The dough should be very thick by now.
7. Add vegan mozzarella to the mixture and stir.
8. Place a safe oven bowl on top of a simmering water pot.
9. Keep stirring the mixture until the cheese melts completely into the flour mixture.
10. Take out the dough and place on 1 (15") sheet of parchment paper.
11. Knead flour dough until the cheese and flour are completely blended.
12. Set the dough in a rectangular shape and cover with 15" of parchment paper.

13. Roll it out and press the dough into roughly 15 by 12-inch rectangle.
14. Remove parchment paper on top.
15. Use the filling from step 1 to top the dough. Leave ½ inch of the dough edges untouched.
16. Evenly top with the raspberry sauce from step 2.
17. Roll the dough into the shape of a log.
18. Divide the log-shaped dough into 8 crosswise pieces and use rolling pins to hold rolls together.
19. Arrange the rolls into the earlier greased pan.
20. Transfer into the heated oven and leave until golden brown. This should take 24-26 minutes.

Lemon Glaze

1. Beat vegan cream cheese and vegan butter in a small bowl until smooth and even.
2. Add lemon extract, sweetener, lemon juice, and vanilla into the small bowl and mix until thoroughly combined.
3. Gradually add 1 tsp of almond milk into the cheese mixture and whisk until well combined.
4. Serve lemon glaze with rolls and enjoy.

Nutrition Facts

Serves: 8 Servings / Calories: 374kcal / Fat: 14g / Carbohydrates: 58g / Protein: 7g

KETO SUMPTUOUS OATS

A ligh and healty dish that can also be served for breakfast. Tasty, quick, and 100% keto!

Ingredients

- 3-4 drops liquid stevia
- 1 tbsp chia seed
- 1/2 tsp vanilla extract
- Pinch Himalayan rock salt, finely ground
- 2/3 cup full-fat coconut milk (+ additional for later use)
- 1/2 cup hemp hearts

Top With (If desired)

- 12 whole almonds
- 6 whole raspberries

Instructions

1. Pour all ingredients into a large container with a lid.
2. Stir until well mixed.
3. Transfer the covered container to the refrigerator for at least 8 hours or leave overnight until it solidifies.
4. Remove the container from the refrigerator and add the reserved milk as desired.
5. Top with desired toppings.
6. Left overs can last up to 2 days if refrigerated.

Nutrition Facts

Serving: 1serving / Calories: 250kcal /
Carbohydrates: 16g / Protein: 8g / Fat: 17g

MUSHROOMS STUFFED WITH VEGAN "BACON" BITS & CREAM CHEESE

Thanks to a filling with cream cheese, smoked tempeh bacon, and chives, these vegan mushrooms are incredibly addictive. Great for snacking, but you can eat a snack too!

Ingredients

- 12 whole fresh mushrooms (cleaned with a damp towel, stems broken off, chopped finely and tight end discarded)
- 2 tablespoons vegan soy bacon bits
- 1/4 teaspoon cayenne pepper, ground
- 1 tablespoon garlic, minced
- 1 tablespoon vegetable oil
- 1/4 teaspoon onion powder
- 8 ounces vegan cream cheese
- 1/4 teaspoon black pepper, ground

Instructions

1. Set your oven to 350°F.
2. Prepare a baking sheet.
3. Put oil into a skillet on medium heat.
4. Sauté the mushroom stems and the garlic in the hot oil for about 2 minutes, until soft.

5. Transfer into mixing bowl and leave to cool.
6. Add the cayenne pepper, vegan soy bacon bits, onion powder, vegan cream cheese, and pepper into the mushroom bowl.
7. Mix until completely blended.
8. Cover the mushroom caps with the stuffing from the mixing bowl.
9. Arrange mushroom caps on baking sheet and place into the oven.
10. Bake for 20 minutes.
11. Serve and enjoy.

Nutrition Facts

Serves: 12 servings / Calories 51kcal / Fat 4g / Carbohydrate 1g / Protein 2g

SUMPTUOUS OLIVE & MUNG BEAN BALLS

These Mung Bean and Olive balls consist of beans, olives, veggies and more. It can be eaten with whole grain pasta or vegetables as a simple meal with loved ones.

Ingredients

- 1/2 cup (finely chopped) California black ripe olives
- 1 minced garlic clove
- 1/4 tsp black pepper, freshly ground
- 1/4 tsp red chili flakes
- 1/4 tsp salt
- 1/2 cup (finely chopped) white onion
- 2 tbsps tomato sauce (sugar-free)
- 2 tbsps chopped sun dried tomatoes (not in oil)
- 1 tsp oregano, dried
- 1/4 cup chopped fresh parsley
- 1 + 1/2 cups mung beans, cooked
- 1 tbsp flaxseed, ground

Instructions

1. Preheat oven to 350°F.
2. Add flaxseed and 3 tbsps of water in a mixing bowl and leave to sit for at least 10 minutes.
3. Crush your cooked mung beans with potato masher or fork until smooth and lumpless.

4. Add tomato sauce, parsley, garlic, spices, onion, sun dried tomatoes, and olives to the mashed beans and stir until mixed.
5. Pour the flaxseed and water mixture into the bean mixture and stir until completely blended.
6. Use hands to mold the bean mixture into 1 + 1/2 balls.
7. Arrange bean balls on your prepared baking sheet.
8. Transfer the baking sheet into the oven and leave for 20 minutes.
9. Turn the sides and bake for 10 more minutes.
10. Now remove bean balls from the oven.
11. They should be slightly brown if adequately cooked.
12. Eat with veggies or pasta.

Nutrition Facts

Serving: 4 balls / Calories 70 calories / Fat 3.5 grams / Carbohydrates 7 grams / Protein 3 grams

BAKED CRISPY AVOCADO FRIES

The biggest secret to this recipe is using the best Avocados. Ripe but not over ripe. Peel off the outer skin, so they are not too mushy.

Ingredients

- Salt, as needed
- 1/2 cup almond flour
- Additional spices, as desired
- 1/4 cup any favorite vegan milk (can be almond milk, coconut milk)
- 1 ripe avocado (peeled, pitted & sliced into fry-sized wedges)
- Pepper, as needed

Instructions

1. Preheat oven to 425°F.
2. Lay out a baking sheet lined with parchment paper.
3. Immerse avocado slices in vegan milk, then roll in almond flour.
4. Transfer to the baking sheet.
5. Lightly season the avocado with salt and pepper.
6. Transfer into oven and bake for a total of 20 minutes, 10 minutes for each side.
7. It's ready to eat and enjoy.

Nutrition Facts

Serves: 1 Serving / Calories: 226kcal /
Carbohydrates: 18g / Protein: 5g / Fat: 16g

VEGETARIAN KETO SNACK RECIPES

A full snack can be really useful when you're out and about. Use this list of vegetarian keto alternatives for a healty and tastfull break.

VEGAN BAGEL THINS

These keto bagels are low carb, egg-free, gluten-free, dairy-free and nut-free and can be eaten as breakfast.

Ingredients

- 1/2 cup psyllium husk powder
- 1 teaspoon salt
- 3 tablespoons flaxseed, ground
- 1 teaspoon baking powder
- Sesame seeds
- 1 cup water
- 1/2 cup tahini, unsalted
- Garnish With (If desired)

Instructions

1. Preheat an oven to 375°F.
2. Pour baking powder, psyllium husk powder, and ground flax seeds and salt taste into a fairly large mixing bowl.
3. Whisk until well blended.
4. Add water to the mix and whisk until water is totally absorbed.
5. Add the tahini and whisk until thoroughly blended You may use clean hands to knead properly.
6. Make thick patty-shapes and cut a small circle in the middle.
7. Arrange patties onto a baking tray.

8. Add sesame seeds and place them into the oven till golden brown. This should take about 40 minutes.
9. Slice into 2 and fill as desired.

Nutrition Facts

Serves: 8 servings / Calories: 292.6kcal / Carbohydrates: 18.2g / Protein: 8.6g / Fat: 22.1g

TACO TURNIP FRIES

This spicy, tasty snack is hugely suggested for individuals who enjoy fried food. Turnip is used to substitute starchy potatoes and to produce still beautiful fries.

Ingredients

Home-made Vegan Taco Seasoning

- 1 teaspoon organic garlic powder
- 1 + 1/2 teaspoons organic onion powder
- 1 + 1/2 tablespoons organic cumin, ground
- 2 tablespoons organic chili powder
- 1/2 teaspoon organic oregano, dried

Turnip

- 1/4 cup organic light olive oil
- 2 tablespoons home-made vegan taco seasoning (see above)
- 2 teaspoons unrefined sea salt, or as needed
- 2 pounds organic turnips (washed, pat dried, peeled & sliced into 1/2" thick sticks)

Instructions

1. Add all taco seasoning ingredients into small

206

bowl and mix until evenly blended.
2. Preheat oven up to 350°F.
3. Put turnip fries inside a ziplock bag and add salt, olive oil, and the home-made vegan taco seasoning.
4. Fasten the ziplock bag and shake vigorously until turnip fries are well coated.
5. Take out turnip fries from the ziplock and transfer to a baking sheet lined with parchment. Make sure there's room, so the chips don't touch.
6. Move baking sheet into a preheated oven and bake until cooked, for up to 25 minutes.
7. Serve with sugar-free ketchup or any other vegan creamy dip.

Nutrition Facts

Serves: 4-6 servings / Net carbs 7.7 grams / Protein 1.7 grams / Fat 9.5 grams / Calories 129 kcal

MUSHROOM CHIPS

These yummy homemade mushroom chips create a healthy option to potato chips. They're like extra-flavored potato chips and are easy to make.

Ingredients

- 4 tablespoons melted coconut oil
- 1/2 teaspoon pink Himalayan salt
- Dash freshly ground black pepper
- 600g (10.6 oz) Portobello mushrooms (mandolin or knife sliced)

Instructions

1. Heat oven up to 300°F.
2. Line a baking tray with the nonstick baking sheet then add mushroom slices.
3. Cover mushroom slices with coconut oil and add salt and freshly ground pepper to taste.
4. If desired, add garlic or chili powder to make spicier.
5. Arrange mushrooms slices onto the baking sheet liner tray and transfer it into a preheated oven.
6. Move baking tray around twice or thrice to ensure even baking.
7. Leave for up to 45-60 minutes, until golden brown and crispy.

8. Let it cool chips before serving.

Nutrition Facts

Serves: 4 servings / Calories 113kcal / Fat 11.7g /
Carbs 0.4g / Protein 1.5g

MATCHA STRAWBERRY PUDDING

This delicious chia pudding is made of 4 essential ingredients and is very healthy for a dessert.

Ingredients

- Stevia or raw honey to taste
- 1 + 1/2 tbsps chia seeds
- 1/2 tsp matcha powder
- 3/4 cup coconut milk
- 2 (minimally diced) strawberries

Instructions

1. Add chia seeds, matcha powder, stevia or raw honey and coconut milk into a bowl with a lid.
2. After you had secured the lid, shake vigorously for 5-10 seconds until the mixture is fully combined.
3. Pour into a glass and leave in the refrigerator for up to 4 hours.
4. Add the diced strawberries into the pudding until well combined and reserve 1 tsp for topping.
5. Use the reserved 1 tsp as toppings.
6. Serve and enjoy.

Nutrition Facts

Serves: 1 serving / Calories: 420 / Fat: 37 g / Carbohydrates: 20 g / Fiber: 13 g / Protein: 7 g

SPICY VEGAN ZUCCHINI CHIPS

These chips are perfect for a calorie-conscious diet. They're low in carbs and also calories, are a reliable source of healthy potassium and are about 50 kcal per serving.

Ingredients

- 1/2 teaspoon salt
- 1 lime, juiced
- 1 tablespoon coconut oil or olive oil
- 1 tablespoon fresh lime zest

- 2 zucchini, average or 4 baby zucchini (mandolin or knife sliced)
- 1/2-1 teaspoon chili powder

Instructions

1. Preheat oven to 230°F.
2. Add chili pepper, lime zest, and lime juice into the mixing bowl.
3. Stir until well blended.
4. Cover the zucchini slices with the spice mix.
5. Arrange the spiced zucchini slices on a parchment paper, lined on a baking tray.
6. Cover with coconut or olive oil and add salt to taste.
7. Move into the preheated oven and leave until crispy and golden. This should take 45-60 minutes.

Nutrition Facts

Serves: 4 servings / Carbs 3.2 grams /
Protein 1.4 grams / Fat 3.8 grams / Calories 54 kcal

GARLIC & ROSEMARY EGGPLANT CHIPS

This recipe is very low in net carbs & taste great!

Ingredients

- 1 garlic clove
- 2 eggplants, average (sliced into 1/4" thick pieces)
- Salt, as necessary
- 1 tablespoon dried or rosemary
- 3 tablespoons olive oil or melted vegan butter

Instructions

1. Prepare a baking sheet lined with foil or parchment paper.
2. Lay the slices of eggplant on the baking sheet.
3. Add salt as desired and allow to sit for 1hr.
4. Transfer into oven to remove any moisture before baking.
5. Use paper towels to clean excess moisture from eggplant slices.
6. Preheat an oven to 350°F.
7. Add mashed garlic, melted vegan butter and chopped rosemary into a small mixing bowl.
8. Stir to blend and coat slices of eggplant with the oil mixture.
9. Add more salt if desired and transfer into preheated oven.

10. Bake until eggplant is well cooked.

11. Serve warm.

Nutrition Facts

Serves: 4 servings / Carbs 3.9 grams /
Protein 1.3 grams / Fat 11.5 grams / Calories 135 kcal

VEGAN CHOCOLATE PUMPKIN PIE

It can serve as a healthy Thanksgiving pie and can easily become a family favorite.

Ingredients

- 15-20 drops Stevia extract, if desired
- 1/2 cup coconut butter
- 2 tablespoons Swerve or Erythritol, powdered
- 1/4 cup coconut oil
- 2 teaspoons pumpkin pie spice mix
- 2 tablespoons coconut oil
- 1/2 cup pumpkin puree, unsweetened
- 100g (85% cocoa solids or more) extra dark chocolate

Instructions

1. In a double boiler, add cocoa oil and chocolate to medium-heat and melt.
2. Take out the heat and let go of the chocolate oil mix.
3. In 18 mini muffin cups add 2 tsp of chocolate. Divide any remainders among the cups of muffin.
4. For 10 minutes or more, transfer the chocolate to a refrigerator.
5. Into the double bowl over medium heat add pumpkin spice mix, erythritol, cocoa oil, and cocoa butter and freeze too.

6. In the cooked blend, add the pumpkin puree and melt entirely.
7. Remove the cooled cups of muffin.
8. In each cup of mini muffin, add 1 generous tsp of the cocoon/pumpkin mix.
9. Cool 30 minutes or longer.
10. It can be cooled until 7 days, or frozen until 90 days.
11. Serve and enjoy.

Nutrition Facts

Serves: 18 servings / Calories 242kcal / Fat 19 g / Carbohydrate 12 g / Protein 8 g

KETO ROASTED OLIVES

This is an effortless appetizer; a baked olive dish that can be quickly made at the last minute without previous flavor. It's all keto & gluten free.

Ingredients

- 1 cup (4 oz.) {stuffed with pimento, almonds or garlic} green olives
- 1 cup (4 oz.) Kalamata olives, pitted
- 1/4 cup olive oil

- 8-10 peeled, whole garlic cloves
- 1 cup (4 oz.) black olives, pitted
- 1 tbsp Herbes de Provence

Add-Ins

- 1 tsp lemon zest, freshly grated
- 1/4 tsp freshly ground black pepper

- Garnish With (If desired)
- Thyme sprigs and/or fresh rosemary sprigs

Instructions

1. Preheat oven to 425°F.
2. Transfer the Herbes de Provence, olive oil, drained olives, and garlic onto a rimmed baking sheet.
3. Toss until entirely mixed.
4. Move baking sheet to the preheated oven and leave till the olive starts to sizzle and garlic is lightly brown.

5. Stir-bake for the first 10 minutes.
6. Leave the baked olive mixture to cool down.
7. Add freshly ground pepper, grated lemon zest, and the baked olives into a bowl and mix until blended.
8. Use rosemary or thyme sprigs as toppings.
9. Serve warm.

Nutrition Facts

Serves: 8 servings / Calories 71kcal / Fat 7g / Carbohydrate 3g / protein 1g

FLOURLESS CRISPY FLAXSEED WAFFLES

These crispy keto waffles are grain-free and are made of ground flaxseed. It doesn't have flour, sugar, or grains. It's completely keto!

Ingredients

- 1 tbsp fresh herbs or 2 tsp ground cinnamon
- 2 cups golden flaxseed, coarsely ground
- 1/2 cup water
- 1 tbsp baking powder, gluten-free

- 1/3 cup melted coconut oil (Alternatively olive oil or avocado oil)
- 5 flax eggs (5 tbsp flax meal + 15 tbsp hot water)
- 1 tsp sea salt

Fresh Herbs Option

- Parsley
- Thyme

- Rosemary

Instructions

1. Set your waffle maker on medium heat.
2. Add 5 tablespoons of flax meal and 15 tablespoons of hot water. Mix and set aside.
3. Mix flaxseed, sea salt, and baking powder into a big mixing bowl.
4. Whisk until completely mixed and set aside to sit.

5. Pour water, oil and flax eggs into a food processor and blend until thoroughly mixed.
6. Transfer the flax egg mixture into a large bowl and stir until fluffy.
7. Let the mixture sit for 3 minutes then stir in the ground cinnamon.
8. Distribute mixture into four places.
9. Ladle portions of batter into the waffle maker and tighten the lid. Cook a portion at a time.
10. Leave to cook until waffle maker beeps.
11. Serve as soon as ready or keep in the refrigerator for some weeks.

Nutrition Facts

Serves: 4 servings / Calories: 550kcal / Fat: 42 g / Carbs: 18.4 g / Protein: 18.3 g

RASPBERRY CHEESECAKE CANDY

This cheesecake with delightful raspberry is delicious and fluffy. This recipe is sugar-free and absolutely indicate for low-carb diets.

Ingredients

- 250g creamed coconut milk
- 15-20 drops liquid stevia if desired
- 1/2 cup almond flour
- 2 tablespoons powdered Swerve or Erythritol
- 1/2 teaspoon vanilla bean powder (Alternatively 1 teaspoon no-sugar vanilla extract)
- 1 cup frozen raspberries
- 1/4 cup coconut flour

Coat With

- 80g extra dark chocolate - 85%-90% cocoa solids
- 4 g coconut oil

Instructions

1. In the electric blender, add frozen raspberries, vanilla, erythritol, and creamy coconut milk.
2. Mix until soft and fluffy.
3. Fill the mixer with almond meal and coconut meal.
4. Mix until blended carefully.
5. Mixing of Scoops on an ice rack.

6. 45 to 60 minutes freeze.
7. In a double boiler, thermally warm the coconut oil and dark chocolate until baked.
8. Let it sleep until fully refreshed.
9. Remove the ice cabinet from the freezer and cover the candy with the chilled chocolate blend with the fork or wooden stick.
10. Fully solidified, cover the candy.
11. Transfer covered candy to a parchment paper cover, lined and cool for a minimum of 15 minutes before serving.
12. Maintain for 7 days in a refrigerator or freezer up to 90 days.

Nutrition Facts

Serves: 16 servings / Calories: 416kcal / Carbohydrates: 6g / Protein: 11g / Fat: 39g

VEGAN FUDGESICLES

These keto Fudgesicles differ from homemade ice pops because they're very creamy while being vegan at the same time. The secret ingredients that make it yummy are healthy almonds.

Ingredients

- 1 can full-fat coconut milk
- Chocolate Drizzle
- 1 teaspoon Erythritol or swerve
- 28g 100% dark unsweetened chocolate
- 1/4 cup + 1 tablespoon granulated Swerve
- Popsicle
- 2 tablespoons coconut oil
- Pinch of salt
- 4 tablespoons cacao powder
- 1/3 cup + 1 tablespoon raw cacao powder

Top With (If Desired)

- Almonds, sliced
- Hemp seeds
- Goji berries
- Freeze-dried berries
- Cacao nibs
- Bee pollen
- Chia seeds

Instructions

1. Add a pinch of salt, swerve, chocolate, coconut milk and cacao powder into a pot over medium heat.

2. Stir and cook until melted.
3. Set aside until it cools.
4. Share the cooled mixture into 6 popsicle molds.
5. Place into the freezer and freeze till solid.
6. Remove frozen popsicles from popsicle molds and place them on with a parchment-lined baking sheet.
7. Heat coconut oil on medium to low heat and add swerve and cacao powder.
8. Drizzle over all the popsicles.
9. Add toppings of your choice.
10. Transfer coated popsicles into a well-covered, large container and put parchment paper in between popsicle layers.
11. Eat immediately or refrigerate.

Nutrition Facts

Serves: 6 servings / Calories 194kcal / Fat 8g / Carbohydrates 28g / Protein 3g

COOKIE DOUGH TRUFFLES

These low-carb truffles are really easy to prepare and are as yummy as chocolate chip cookies. Besides, they are low in carbs and have healthy fats. It's just what you need.

Ingredients

Truffles

- 1/4 teaspoon salt
- 2-ounce dark chocolate, chopped (ideally 85-90%)
- 1/4 cup Swerve or Erythritol, powdered
- 1/2 cup coconut flour
- 1 cup almond butter, toasted
- 1/2 cup pecans or walnuts, chopped
- 1 teaspoon vanilla powder or cinnamon

Coat With

- 1-ounce coconut oil or cacao butter
- 2 + 1/2 ounce dark chocolate, (ideally 85-90%)

Instructions

1. Add chopped dark chocolate, vanilla powder or cinnamon, salt, pecans or walnuts, powdered Erythritol, and almond butter into a mixing bowl.
2. Add coconut flour to the dough and stir until properly mixed.

225

3. Place dough into a refrigerator for 1hour.
4. Make 16 truffle-shapes from the chilled dough and transfer to a tray.
5. Put in a freezer for 1hour.
6. Melt dark chocolate and cacao butter in a glass bowl over a water-filled saucepan placed on medium heat.
7. Take away from heat and let sit till it cools.
8. Use a fork or wooden stick to coat cookies with the melted chocolate.
9. Immerse cookies in chocolate until it thickens.
10. Trickle leftover chocolate on cookies.
11. Place coated cookies onto a tray lined with paper parchment. Refrigerate for about 15 minutes before serving.
12. It can be conserved in the fridge for up to 1 week and can be frozen for up to 90 days.

Nutrition Facts

Serves: 16 truffles / Carbs 3.4 grams /
Protein 5 grams / Fat 16.2 grams / Calories 200 kcal

TRICOLOR KETO VEGAN PARFAITS

These parfaits are perfect for a quick-prep dessert. Vanilla coconut cream serves as a topping for the red strawberry layer and is finished with fresh blueberries.

Ingredients

Red layer

- 1/3 cup water
- 1-2 tablespoons Swerve or Erythritol (Alternatively 15-20 drops liquid stevia)
- 1 + 1/2 cups fresh strawberries (Alternatively frozen & thawed)
- 1 tablespoon chia seeds

Blue layer

- 3/4 cup (fresh or frozen) blueberries or blackberries

White layer

- 3/4 cup coconut cream
- 1-2 teaspoons no-sugar vanilla extract (Alternatively 1/2 teaspoon vanilla powder)
- 1/2 cup liquid coconut milk
- 15-20 drops liquid stevia (Alternatively 2 tablespoons Swerve or powdered erythritol)

Instructions

1. Add strawberries and 1/4 water into a high speed blender or food processor.

2. Blend until smooth.
3. Pour blended strawberry and stevia into a saucepan.
4. Add remaining water and chia seeds and then transfer all into the strawberry and stevia mixture.
5. Warm the mixture slightly.
6. Transfer strawberry mixture into 4 glasses and place it into the refrigerator for 1 hour until solid.
7. Add coconut cream, vanilla, coconut milk, and powdered erythritol into a bowl.
8. Using an immersion blender, process the mixture until airy and smooth.
9. Scoop and distribute the same amount of white layer into the 4 glasses already filled with the strawberry layer.
10. Use fresh or frozen blueberries as toppings.
11. Immediately serve and eat it or you can refrigerate for 3 days.

Nutrition Facts

Serves: 4 servings / Carbs 8.9 grams /
Protein 3.7 grams / Fat 22 grams / Calories 244 kcal

TRICOLOR BERRY POPSICLES

This is a summer food idea. Crushed ice and berries added to colorful fruit popsicles over marble background.

Ingredients

Red layer

- 1 + 3/4 cups (fresh or frozen & thawed) strawberries
- 15-20 drops liquid stevia (if desired)
- 1/4 cup water

Blue layer

- 15-20 drops liquid stevia
- 1 + 1/2 cup (fresh or frozen) wild blueberries
- 2 tablespoons fresh lemon juice

White layer

- 1/2 cup coconut cream
- 2 tablespoons Swerve or powdered erythritol, or added as necessary
- 1-2 teaspoon no-sugar vanilla extract or ½ teaspoons vanilla powder
- 1/2 cup liquid coconut milk
  1 tablespoon fresh lemon juice

Instructions

Red Layer

1. Add strawberries and 1/4 cup of water into a food processor or blender.
2. Blend until very smooth.
3. Distribute strawberry puree into 10 popsicle molds.
4. Freeze for about 1-2 hours.

Blue Layer

1. Add blueberries, lemon juice, and stevia into a food processor or electric blender.
2. Process until smooth and leave to sit.

White Layer

1. Add cream cheese, lemon juice, coconut cream, powdered erythritol and vanilla into mixing bowl.
2. Blend until a smooth consistency is achieved.
3. Whisk with a hand whisker or electric mixer.
4. Layer the white cheesecake over the red layer (strawberry layer).
5. Top everything with the blue layer (the blueberry).
6. Freeze until solid.
7. Add warm water into a tall pot and dip the popsicle mold into the water for 15-20 seconds.
8. Wrap into plastic bags and refrigerate up to 6 months.

Nutrition Facts

Serves: 10 popsicles / Calories 44kcal / Protein 0.3g /
Fat 0.2g / Carbohydrate 11g

KETOGENIC NUTELLA

This spread is a homemade paleo and keto Nutella hazelnut that is absolutely decadent! Extremely rich and chocolatey, it is delicious and healthy at the same time. You'll never miss the carb-filled ones.

Ingredients

- Few drops liquid stevia, as necessary (if desired)
- 1/2 cup warm coconut milk (if desired)
- 1 bar (85-90% cacao) dark chocolate
- 1 tablespoon coconut oil
- 1/2 cup almonds

- 1-2 teaspoon no-sugar vanilla extract or 1/2 teaspoon vanilla powder
- 2 tablespoons Swerve or powdered Erythritol
- 1 tablespoon cacao powder
- 1 cup hazelnuts, peeled 1 cup macadamia nuts

Instructions

1. Preheat oven till 375°F.
2. Spread out hazelnuts, almonds and macadamia nuts on a baking sheet.
3. Transfer into the preheated oven and leave until it turns light brown.
4. Bring out of the oven and leave to cool for 15 minutes.

5. Meanwhile, pour chocolate and coconut oil into a heatproof bowl.
6. Place chocolate and coconut oil mixture in a pot with boiling water and stir until completely melted.
7. Use a food processor to smash the macadamia nuts until a smooth consistency is achieved.
8. Pour cacao powder, powdered erythritol, coconut oil, vanilla powder, and the melted chocolate into the food processor.
9. Process until completely mixed and combined.
10. Add trickles of warm coconut milk, into the mix and process till combined.
11. Pour into a jar and leave to cool.
12. Refrigerate for up to 7 days. If coconut milk was not added, it could last for up to 90 days.

Nutrition Facts

Serves: 2 cups / Calories 86kcal / Fat 8g / Carbohydrates 3g / Protein 2g

KETOGENIC ICE-CREAM (CHOCOLATE FLAVOR)

This low carb and dairy-free keto ice cream is suitable for everyone, whether you're on a keto diet or not!

Ingredients

- 1/2 cup + 1 tablespoon 100% pure dark chocolate
- 6 drops chocolate stevia
- 1/4 teaspoons clear stevia drops, or as necessary
- 1 can chill coconut cream or icy coconut milk

Instructions

1. Pour all ingredients into a large bowl.
2. By using an electric mixer, process the ingredients until they are smooth, bubbly, and thick.
3. Pour mixture into an ice cream maker and follow the manual's instructions.
4. Eat once ready or you may also freeze and then thaw until it is eatable (It will be slightly solid when kept in the refrigerator).

Nutrition Facts

Serves: 4 servings / Calories 184kca / Fat 19.1g / Carbohydrates 4.4g / Protein 1.8g

KETOGENIC CURLY CHOCOLATE POTS

These simple keto chocolate pots are extremely easy and quick to make yet have all the qualities and benefits of a genuinely decadent pudding. The creamy avocado and no refined sugar make it ridiculously healthy for you despite being so delicious.

Ingredients

- 1/3 cup raw cacao powder
- 3/4 teaspoon liquid stevia
- Chocolate curls
- 2 tablespoons coconut butter (soft not melted) or coconut oil
- 2 + 1/2 (pitted & peeled) large avocados
- 1/2 cup raw cacao powder
- 2/3 teaspoon liquid stevia
- Pinch sea salt
- 1 teaspoon vanilla powder
- 15g cocoa butter
- 1-2 tablespoons cashew or almond milk, unsweetened

Instructions

1. Add all ingredients into a mixing bowl.
2. By using an immersion blender, mix until a smooth consistency is achieved.

3. Transfer blended the mixture into yogurt pots.
4. Pour cocoa butter into a jug or an oven bowl.
5. Place cocoa butter into a pan on medium heat and add 1" of water.
6. When cocoa butter is completely melted, set aside.
7. Pour melted butter into a fresh bowl and add stevia and cacao powder.
8. Stir and check for desired sweetness, then let sit.
9. With a palette knife, spread the butter mixture on a tile or marble surface.
10. Leave to solidify but sticky to the touch.
11. Use your scraper to create flakes or chocolate curls.
12. It's ready for consumption and can be refrigerated for about 4 days.

Nutrition Facts

Serves: 4 servings / Carbs 6.3 grams /
Protein 6 grams / Fat 31.3 grams / Calories 339 kcal

VEGAN COCONUT BARS

This healthy 3-Ingredient Vegan Coconut Crack Bars recipe is just what you need to satisfy your sweet craving. Totally sugar-free, these low carb and keto-friendly coconut bars can get you addicted in no time, and take only a few minutes to prepare!

Ingredients

- 10-20 saffron threads
- 3.5 ounces vegan butter or coconut oil
- 1 + 1/3 cup coconut milk, unsweetened
- 4 tablespoons Erythritol
- 1 + 3/4 cups unsweetened coconut, shredded
- 1 teaspoon cardamom powder

Top With (If Desired)

- Almonds, chopped

Instructions

1. Add 1 + 1/4 cup coconut milk into a bowl.
2. Add shredded coconut to the milk.
3. Mix until totally combined then set aside for up to 30 minutes.
4. Add the saffron threads, erythritol, and the leftover coconut milk into the bowl.
5. Stir and make sure the sweetener is totally mixed and well combined.

6. Pour coconut oil or add vegan butter into another bowl over low heat until it's totally melted.
7. Add the coconut mix into the melted oil or butter.
8. Keep stirring to turn coconut mixture to paste. Stir cook for about 7 minutes.
9. Pour cardamom powder into the mixture and let it cook for 5 more minutes.
10. Grease your baking tray with oil or butter and spread the coconut mixture on the baking tray. Make it up to 1 cm thick.
11. Let it cool for a while, then transfer to the freezer and leave for 2 hours to 2 hours 30 minutes.
12. Slice coconut bar into small squares or any preferred shape, and it is ready to be served.
13. It can be left in a refrigerator for up to 5 days to solidify.
14. It can be edible up to 90 days if placed in the freezer.

Nutrition Facts

Serves: 15 servings / Calories: 108kcal / Carbohydrates: 2g / Protein: 2g / Fat: 11g

CINNAMON AND CARDAMOM FAT BOMBS

Small but tasty. This is the ideal snack and works well with a cup of coffee or tea with the great scents of Vanilla, cinnamon, and cardamom.

Ingredients

- 1/2 tsp vanilla extract
- 1/4 tsp ground cardamom (green)
- 3 oz. unsalted butter
- 1/2 cup unsweetened shredded coconut
- 1/4 tsp ground cinnamon

Instructions

1. Put the butter at room temperature.
2. Carefully roast the crushed coconut, with moderate heat, and brown it gently. This gives you a delightful taste, but if you wish, you can save it. Let cool.
3. In a pan, mix butter, cocoa halves, and spices accurately together. Chill for about 5-10 minutes in the fridge and until mildly firm.
4. Shape into pieces of the walnut size. Roll the bones into the rest of the cocoon nuts.
5. Keep in a fridge or freezer.

Nutrition Facts

Serves: 10 servings / Calories: 90kcal /
Carbohydrates: 0.4g / Protein: 0.4g / Fat: 10g

SPICY DEVILED EGGS

Delicious fried eggs from curry paste with heat and flavor. An ideal snack or holiday appetizer.

Ingredients

- 6 eggs
- 1/2 cup mayonnaise
- 1/2 tbsp poppy seeds
- 1/4 tsp salt
- 1 tbsp red curry paste

Instructions

1. Insert the eggs into a bowl, in hot water, just sufficient water to cover the eggs. Without a lid bring to a boil.
2. Allow the eggs to cook for approximately a week. In ice-cold water cool rapidly.
3. Eggshells should be removed. Divide the egg into half, cut it off from both sides. Cut out the egg yolk, put it in a little jar.
4. On a tray, place the egg whites and let rest in the cooler.
5. Mix in a soft batter curry paste, mayonnaise, and egg yolks. Salt to flavor. Salt to flavor.
6. Please remove the egg whites and add the batter.
7. Spray the seeds and serve.

Nutrition Facts

Serves: 6 servings / Calories: 200kcal /
Carbohydrates: 1g / Protein: 6g / Fat: 19g

PUMPKIN SPICE LATTE

Whip that slurpy latte up and feel the coffee and pumpkin love in a great warm hug. A perfect fall or at any time snack. You want this!

Ingredients

- 1 tsp pumpkin pie spice
- 1 cup boiling water
- 2 tsp instant coffee powder
- 1 oz. unsalted butter

Instructions

1. In a deep pan, put butter, spices, and instant coffee to use with an immersion blender. Alternatively, the components can be placed straight in the mixer container.
2. Add boiling water, and mix until a thin liquid is created for 20–30 seconds.
3. Sprinkle a cup with some cinnamon or pumpkin spice. Serve right away!
4. It is even tastier with heavy cream whipped on top.

Nutrition Facts

Serves: 1 servings / Calories: 216kcal / Carbohydrates: 1g / Protein: 0.5g / Fat: 23g

Printed in Great Britain
by Amazon

60448294R00149